Orioles' Big Bird

Mark Trumbo speaks softly, but carries a big stick

By Peter Schmuck

BACK STORY PUBLISHING, LLC
www.backstorypublishing.com

Orioles' Big Bird
Mark Trumbo speaks softly, but carries a big stick

by Peter Schmuck

Copyright © 2018 by Back Story Publishing, LLC

All rights reserved. No part of this book may be reproduced, scanned, or stored in any printed, mechanical, or electronic form, or distributed or held or stored for distribution by any physical or electronic means, without written permission from Back Story Publishing. Please respect the rights of authors and publishers, and refrain from piracy of copyrighted materials. Thank you.

ISBN: 978-0-9993967-6-6
Library of Congress Control Number: 2018951981

Paperback editions printed in the United States of America. For information on quantity discounts or special editions to be used for educational programs, fundraising, premiums, or sales promotions, please inquire via electronic mail at *admin@BackStoryPublishing.com*, or write to Back Story Publishing, Post Office Box 2580, Rancho Mirage, California 92270 USA.

News media inquiries may be directed to *newsroom@BackStoryPublishing.com*.

Credits
Cover and back cover photographs by Gary Ambrose, copyright © Back Story Publishing, LLC

Designer: Stuart Funk
Back Story Publishing Editorial Director: Ellen Alperstein

www.BackStoryPublishing.com

CONTENTS

INTRODUCTION....................page 6

CHAPTER 1
Yankee Stadium, September 2016 ....page 8

CHAPTER 2
The Pee Wee With Power ....page 12

CHAPTER 3
Little Angel With the Big Arm ....page 19

CHAPTER 4
The Little Leaguer Goes Long ....page 24

CHAPTER 5
Hearing the Beat of the Drum ....page 32

CHAPTER 6
Heaven on the Mound at Angel Stadium ....page 37

CHAPTER 7
The Pros Take Aim ....page 47

CHAPTER 8
A Scholarship or a Paycheck? ....page 55

CHAPTER 9
A Crushing Blow .... page 61

CHAPTER 10
Welcome to Utah .... page 67

CHAPTER 11
Back to Baseball School .... page 72

CHAPTER 12
Figuring Out Failure .... page 81

CHAPTER 13
A Detour to the Dominican Republic .... page 86

CHAPTER 14
On Wings of an Angel .... page 90

CHAPTER 15
The Show Stoppers .... page 95

CHAPTER 16
Leading With His Heart .... page 102

CHAPTER 17
Sun, Rain, and a Swing Change .... page 109

CHAPTER 18
The Oriole Soars Into Home Run History .... page 117

AFTERWORD .... page 128

MARK TRUMBO — BY THE NUMBERS .... page 134

GLOSSARY OF BASEBALL TERMS .... page 136

INTRODUCTION

Albert Einstein dropped out of school when he was 15. Michael Jordan was cut from his high school basketball team. Walt Disney was fired from his first job because his boss thought he had no imagination.

Even if people call you the smartest person in the world, even if you're the best basketball player ever, even if you're the guy who invented Mickey Mouse, sometimes you fail.

This book is about Mark Trumbo. He's a baseball player who hit more home runs in 2016 than any other major league player. He's not as well-known as the legendary Babe Ruth or even his former Baltimore Orioles' teammate, Manny Machado, but he has reached the top of a difficult game.

If you don't know who he is, why should you read about him? Because, like a lot of famous and successful people, Mark has known failure. And that makes a good story.

He was born with talent, and has worked hard since he was 6 years old to make the most of it. But talent and hard work don't always give you a clear path to glory. Sometimes, bad things happen that you can't control, and how you deal with them can help or hurt you. How you deal with them makes you the person you become.

I have been a sportswriter for many years. I have traveled all over the United States, and have gotten to know some of America's best athletes. They all have different stories about how they got to the top of their sports. I wanted to tell Mark's story because, even if you don't know anything about baseball, you can see how someone with a dream found a way around the things that made it hard to come true. Whether your dream is playing centerfield for the New York Yankees, or being the best science teacher ever, you will always find adventure along the way.

Like Mark.

Peter Schmuck

CHAPTER 1

Yankee Stadium, September 2016

On the last Friday night of the regular baseball season, Yankee Stadium was packed with loud New Yorkers. It was their last chance to see their beloved team play this year. The Yankees were out of the playoffs, and, after Sunday, they were headed for the offseason.

Not so for their opponents in this three-game series. The visiting Baltimore Orioles were hanging on to the last spot in the playoffs. To get into the best position, they had to win here, right next to the original stadium known as "The House that Ruth Built." That nickname for the former Yankee Stadium was a tribute to Babe Ruth. He was often called the game's best player, and he was the first really famous one. For nearly 40 years,

Ruth held the record for most home runs in a career — 714. For almost that long, he also held the single-season home run record — 60.

Now, almost 70 years after Babe Ruth died, one Orioles' player had more home runs this season than any other major leaguer — Mark Trumbo. So far in this game, he had made outs in his first two at-bats, the first on a ground ball, the second on a fly. Now, in the fifth inning, it was his turn again to hit. He walked to home plate, scuffed the dirt with his cleats, and took a couple of practice swings. He looked out into the vast outfield. It was like an ocean of green under the bright stadium lights.

Mark was a long way from Southern California, where he grew up watching the local major league team, the California Angels, play in a stadium 15 minutes from his house. Now, standing at home plate in Yankee Stadium, it was almost 25 years since Mark's dad had taken him into the backyard, handed him a tiny bat, and taught him how to hit a baseball. Now, that little boy had become a man with a chance to make history.

The road to the major leagues hadn't been easy for Mark to travel. By the time he was 8, his baseball talent was clear to anyone who saw him play. But after high school, a major injury had forced him to learn a new position, had forced him to move through years of minor league baseball before he ever got here, to what the players call "The Show." Now, he was a star, the home run champion for 2016. He had hit so many homers that year, the Orioles' radio announcer started calling them "Trumbombs."

The pitcher got the signal from the catcher. Mark went into his stance and stared at the mound. Was the pitcher going to throw a fastball? Curveball? Slider? Would Mark be able to see it leave the pitcher's hand in time to read it?

He would. He did. The Yankees pitcher threw a slider that Mark saw coming. He swung hard and connected. The crack of the bat smacking the ball made the crowd groan. It sailed over the wall in left field for a 2-run homer. For Mark, it was Number 47 for the year.

CHAPTER 2

The Pee Wee With Power

If you like to play baseball, or watch other people play, you want to be in Orange County, California. Just south of Los Angeles, it's a warm-weather region that grows good players like Colorado grows mountains.

In this part of Southern California, baseball is played at a high level at every level, from Little League to high school to college to Major League Baseball (MLB).

Mark Trumbo was born in 1986. He grew up in Villa Park, in Orange County, and from the ages of 6 to 11, he played in Villa Park Little League. In high school, he played with and against other boys who would also grow up to play big league baseball, including Phil Hughes, who would pitch for the Yankees in the World Series in 2009. Another local kid, Brad Boxberger, also would become an MLB pitcher, for the Tampa Bay Rays a few years later.

Mark's high school team, the Villa Park Spartans, is a Southern California powerhouse in baseball, and so is the local university, Cal State Fullerton. That city is next to Anaheim, home of the major league Angels.

Mark started playing Little League T-ball as a second-grader at Linda Vista Elementary School. He wanted to be a pitcher. He and his dad, Grant, spent a lot of warm evenings watching major leaguers play at Angel Stadium. Some nights, they could feel the thunder of fireworks going off from Disneyland nearby, lighting up the sky.

When Mark was little, the star pitchers for the Angels were left-handers, and Mark threw right-handed. But Mark was also a good hitter, so at first, his favorite Angel was an outfielder, slugger Tim Salmon.

In 1998, Angel Stadium added a rock formation with a waterfall behind the wall in left centerfield. Sitting in the stands, watching his team, Mark would imagine what it was like to be Tim Salmon, standing at the plate, waiting for a pitch he could knock into the rocks for a home run.

In 2002, when Mark was in high school, the Angels won the World Series behind the pitching of another favorite player, John Lackey. He was a tall, lanky, right-hander. By then, Mark, too, was a tall, right-handed pitcher. He, too, stared down high-school hitters from the mound, just like Lackey.

Mark's best friends were Kurt Gottschling and Dane Ferguson. Mark met Kurt playing T-ball when he was 6. He already knew Dane, whom he met a couple of years earlier, according to Mark and his dad, while they were out walking their dog.

"We were 4 or so, and he followed us home," Mark remembers. "My dad noticed after a while there was this kid who was too young to really know what he's doing, so we turned around and walked him back to his house."

Mark played baseball with and against both of them through Little League, and they all played on the same high school team. Today, they are men in their 30s, and they are still close friends.

Both Kurt and Dane say Mark was the best kid baseball player they ever saw. When other kids were struggling just to hit the ball off the tee, Mark was making solid contact, as if he were born to swing a bat. Even as a 7-year-old, Mark got noticed by adults.

Like other places, coaches for teams in the Villa Park Little League were mostly dads of the players. At the beginning of each season, team coaches would take turns choosing names from a list of kids who had signed up in each age group until everybody had a full team, and there were no more names. The process was similar to how professional teams choose players — that process is called a draft.

Mark was so good that all the Little League coaches wanted to draft him for their team. According to Grant, one season, when he was still in elementary school, Mark's coach from the year before told his new coach, "'If you don't release Mark so I can draft him, I'm going to draft *your* son to play for me.'"

No coach wants his kid playing for another team. That's how Mark ended up playing for the same team two years in a row.

By the time he was in third grade, Mark told his teacher, Brandi Aarvig, that he was going to grow up and play for the California Angels. (The team changed its name a few years ago, and now is called the Los Angeles Angels of Anaheim.)

But he wasn't boasting, he was just stating the truth. In fact, Mark talked very little. He was a shy kid who was more likely to talk about a bad play he made than brag about the home run he just hit.

Mark started playing T-ball about the same time he learned to read.

Recently, Ms. Aarvig remembered what other kids in the class would say when she asked them, "Who are you going to play today?"

"'We're playing Mark's team,'" she remembers them saying. "'We're not going to win.'"

Mark was always tall for his age, and he stood out. He jokes now that all the photos from grade school show him standing in the back row. He also stood out because he was so much better at baseball than anybody else. But his friends, Kurt and Dane, also remember him as a kid who never bragged about himself, and never seemed to be very far from a ballfield.

It was in his blood.

His dad played baseball at the University of Southern California, which is in Los Angeles, and also is considered an historic college baseball power. So Mark had a pretty good coach right at home. Sometimes, his friends joined him in his workouts with Grant.

Both of Mark's parents, Grant and his mom, Debbie, were engineers. That kind of work demands precision, and careful preparation. No surprise, then, that Kurt describes Grant's workouts as "intense."

Grant, Kurt says, "could tell how good Mark was at such a young age, and almost kind of wanted to live through Mark with baseball."

Like Mark, Kurt said the workouts with Grant were tough love. It was tough, but it made you better at what you loved.

"Grant would pick us up in his station wagon and take us down to the field," Kurt remembers. "I was 8 or 9 nine years old, and Grant would hit us ground balls on the Little League infield [from] 60 feet away, and

Mark and his sister, Michelle, Christmas 1992.

hit them as hard as he possibly could. Balls would be bouncing off my chest, me and Mark."

He wasn't doing it to be mean, but to show the boys how hard it is to excel. Kurt says that Grant showed them that you had to "catch the ball or you're going to get hurt. He made us good players."

Still, you wonder what Kurt and Dane's mothers were thinking when their little boys came home from the playground with bruises all over their chests.

At first, Mark's mom, Debbie, thought that the hard drills and long hours would make her little boy burn out on baseball. But like everyone, she learned that her kid was different from most others.

In addition to Little League, Mark went to special baseball camps during the summers. One day, after a long, hot workout at camp, he came home to get ready for a Little League game he had that was starting soon.

"I thought, well, this is when we'll find out just how much he wants to play that game," Debbie recalls thinking that day. "He got home from the game and asked his dad if they could play catch before it got dark."

"When everyone was out skateboarding," Mark remembers, "you could find my dad and me over at the middle school working on the game."

"Even if it was pouring rain," Dane says, "he and his dad were playing catch. He was always getting better."

One day, everybody in Mark's third-grade class at Linda Vista Elementary School made a ceramic tile with their name on it. Nearly 25 years later, a wall at the school is still covered with those tiles, but there's no tile with Mark's name on it. Recently asked about that missing tile, Ms. Aarvig guessed that, knowing Mark, he didn't want to display it for everyone to see.

"He was a big, strong kid," Dane says. But he might have been the quietest. "He was always one of the smarter kids in the class, [but he] was definitely shy."

People knew how special Mark was, how much he loved baseball. They knew he was a quiet, serious kid. What they didn't know until much later was the secret he was keeping about his mom.

CHAPTER 3

The Little Angel With the Big Arm

Both of Mark's parents worked as engineers at the Boeing Aircraft Co. After work and on weekends, Grant would practice baseball skills with Mark and, sometimes, Kurt and Dane. Grant would pitch balls for them to hit, they would play catch, and Grant would make each throw longer and longer to build up their arm muscles.

Mark's ability to hit a baseball at a very young age was matched only by his ability to throw one.

"Pitching," Mark says, "came very naturally. I didn't work on it a lot because that work was easy."

Mark says he was a competitive kid, that he wanted "to win at anything. I think that served me well in a lot of ways, but sometimes I wish I could just turn it off and enjoy the weather."

Nothing stood in the way of baseball, but maybe one reason he worked so hard, one reason he never "turned it off" was because when Mark was 7, his mom came home one day with some awful news. She had breast cancer. Nearly 2 million women around the world get that disease every year, and some of them die from it.

Mark was too little then to understand just how serious his mom's illness was, but he knew she missed a lot of work at Boeing. He knew she had surgery, and many more treatments that made her very weak, and made her forget things.

Kurt and Dane were the only people Mark told that his mom was sick.

"That was something he never talked about," Kurt says now. "Most people — people outside of me and Dane — I'll bet you most people never even knew or still, to this day, probably don't know that his mom was sick. It was something that was never discussed."

Mark's teacher, Ms. Aarvig, didn't know either, at least for a while. When she finally found out, Ms. Aarvig realized that it "was the first time I ever really thought about breast cancer."

She didn't know it then, but 17 years later, she also would get breast cancer. By then, Mark was a major league baseball player. But he remembered her, and was there for Ms. Aarvig, just as he was for his mom.

Today, Mark's old teacher remembers that even though Debbie Trumbo was sick, she was still in-

Top: After T-ball, Mark played on several Villa Park Little League teams, including the Braves. One of the coaches on that team was Mark's dad, Grant, top row, right, and his teammates included his friends Dane, middle row, second from right, and Kurt, kneeling on the right side of the sign. Mark is standing next to Dane, on the end. Bottom: Even as a Little League Angel, Mark's pitching form was impressive.

volved in the lives of her children. Mark always came to school neatly dressed, she says. "He always wore a plaid shirt that was buttoned up. It was tucked in. His hair was always combed. He was so quiet, so well-mannered. He was like the most perfect student you could ever have."

Mark's little sister, Michelle, was only 3 when their mom got sick. Maybe he felt he needed to be strong for her. Even though he was worried, he held his feelings inside. He was too young to understand illness, and medicine, but he understood baseball, so he focused on that.

Luckily, Debbie got better. But it took a long time. Sometimes, cancer comes back, and you have to have treatment all over again. For many years, the family would be torn between periods of worry, and periods of relief.

He's 32 now, but Mark still doesn't like to talk about the part of his life when his mom was sick. "It weighs on you," Mark admits. "It kind of looms in the background, but she always had a good attitude." His mom was positive, and that helped him and his sister get through the bad times.

Debbie recently said that it was difficult to know how her illness affected Mark because he was so shy, and hid his feelings. She believes that baseball helped him through those tough childhood years.

"He was so big on baseball," she says. "I just remember more that my daughter was 3 years old. She was such a little girl, … and it really upset her when I was in the hospital."

Baseball, Mark says, was a way to bond with his mom when she was sick. He couldn't make her well, but he could keep her spirits up with reports about his success. While she was stuck at home, recovering from a treatment, Mark would come back from every game he played with a full report.

"When you're a kid," he says, "you don't really know what's going on. You just know that mom's sick. You just try to provide support. But I think she took a lot of joy hearing about the baseball things I was doing. … I think that always brought a smile to her face."

By the time Mark was 10, Debbie seemed to have beaten the cancer. But in 2011, when he was 25, it came back. She continues to undergo treatment today. And she continues to take pride in Mark's achievements.

CHAPTER 4

The Little Leaguer Goes Long

Mark played in the Villa Park Little League for five years. By the time he finished his final Little League season, he was a local legend. He was 11 years old, and he had the power of a high school player.

In those days, two of the league's fields were separated from the street by two fences. They were about 25 feet apart, with grass in between. The far fence bordered the sidewalk along the street.

Grant Trumbo has a lot of memories of Mark playing on those fields. And they're not all about the action during the games.

"Batting practice at the Little League level," Grant remembers, "there were more kids standing on the other side of the fence to retrieve Mark's batting practice balls than were on the side of the fence where Mark was hitting from."

That was odd — almost nobody who was only 10 or 11 was able to hit a ball far enough to clear the first fence, much less the grass.

Everybody who knew anything about Villa Park baseball knew the Mark Trumbo home run story. Depending on who tells it, the details vary. But everybody knows that a certain home run he hit when he was 11 was special.

More than 20 years after it happened, Kurt Gottschling remembers it as if it were yesterday.

It was Mark's last year in Little League. He was playing a game in the league's larger field along the fences. The fence closest to the field, Kurt recalls, "was about 220 feet [away from home plate], and beyond the right field fence, there was a grass area for another 20 or 30 feet. Then another fence, and the street. Across the street was a house, so we're talking another 100 feet beyond the Little League fence. I had never seen anyone even get it past the fence."

Mark was up to bat. He swung at the pitch, and the ball flew off the bat, Kurt says, "over the fence, over the street, and onto the roof of that house … probably 320 feet."

Mark's dad remembers what might have been the first "Trumbomb" a bit differently. He says the ball hit the roof of the house, bounced over, and landed in the backyard swimming pool.

Mark told *his* version of the story to ESPN a couple of years ago. He remembers that the ball cleared the two fences, and hit a car parked on the street. He estimated that the ball traveled 230 feet. That distance is still a huge poke for a kid that age, but modest Mark has a habit of playing down his achievements. The ball probably went farther.

What is not in dispute is that the house across the street belongs to the same people today who lived there in 1997. They are the Christensens, and Karen Christensen recently said that balls occasionally landed in the family swimming pool, whether they were hit by Mark or someone else. Probably, that someone else hit the ball when they were standing closer to the fence than to home plate. Karen still keeps a box of baseballs in a cabinet on the patio that they fished out of their pool. They look pretty old.

Today, the trees along the street have grown so tall and thick that not many baseballs get over or through them. And before the Christensens remodeled the part of the house closest to the street several years ago, sometimes balls flying from across the street broke the kitchen window. In fact, she says, one actually got stuck in the middle of a window without even breaking it!

"They made windows better then," she says.

Mark still claims that most of the damage he did as a Little Leaguer was to the cars parked on the street behind the fence. "I think I broke several windows of

Top: Mark was famous for hitting long balls over the outfield fence of this Little League field in Orange County. Bottom: The trees weren't as tall then, and once, he hit a home run over the fence, across the street, and into Karen Christensen's pool. Karen, pictured, and her husband, Jim, still live in that house, just visible under the trees in the background on the right of the top photo.

parked cars out in that street," he says.

The big home run into the Christensen's pool was one of Mark's last feats of glory in Little League. He stopped playing there after that year because Grant thought he needed a higher level of competition. So instead of playing strictly with local kids his own age, Mark would "play up" on various travel and tournament teams.

When Mark was 12, one of those teams traveled to New York to play in a tournament at Dreams Park in Cooperstown. It's in the same town as the Baseball Hall of Fame, about a mile away.

Every summer, Dreams Park draws hundreds of teams of 12-year-old players from all over the country, usually 106 teams every week for 13 weeks. In 1998, Mark's Orange County team, the Okeiki Warriors, won the weekly title. It's a big deal, because a team must play at least 10 games that week to take top honors, including three or four playoff games.

The day before the tournament starts, individual players participate in skills competitions. Mark won the home run contest, and received a huge trophy as his reward. He also was named MVP of that week's tournament.

Other kids from Orange County also have done well at Dreams Park, which is known as a proving ground for future baseball talent. The facility is huge, with 22 fields, and one of the main public dining areas has walls lined with photos of some of the kids who played

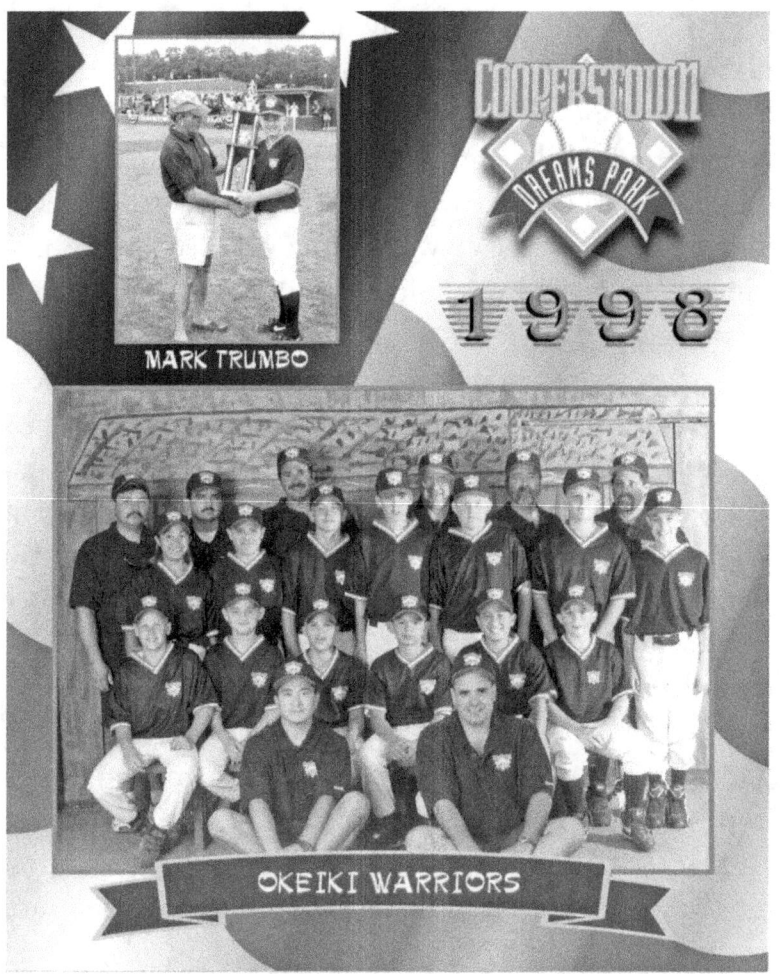

When he was 12, Mark won the home run trophy, and his team, the Okeiki Warriors, won the weekly tournament at a national competition in Cooperstown, New York.

here, and who went on to play in the major leagues. Today, one of those photos is of a teammate of Mark's, when he was with the Angels — Mike Trout, who is widely known as the best player in baseball.

Mark continued to play on those travel teams until he got to high school, but he wasn't always the big bopper.

During middle school, Mark began to struggle at the plate. He still could throw the ball harder than ever, but hitting no longer was automatic. It was the first time he ever really felt like a failure on the baseball diamond.

Part of Mark's middle-school slump might have been because, finally, he was like most boys. Around 11 or 12, many boys hit a growth spurt that makes them feel like their body is a stranger, like they're living in someone else's body. Suddenly everything seems different. The bat feels lighter. Suddenly, the other kid pitchers are much better, throwing harder, they're throwing different kinds of pitches.

Between his last Little League game at 11, and his first day in high school, at 14, Mark grew almost a foot.

Mark had skipped Little League at the time most of those players were hitting the same growth spurt, so he didn't have a chance to adjust. Suddenly, he was playing against older kids who had learned to live with their changing bodies. They had grown past the point where Mark seemed to be stuck.

But one thing would save him. One thing would restore his confidence. That thing was all those years of Grant's tough love. All those early years they spent grinding out the basics of the game. Mark didn't know it at the time, but he was learning a valuable lesson when he was practicing while the other boys were skateboarding. Hard work pays off. In a few years, after another setback, he would remember that lesson. And it would be his ticket to The Show.

Before he started high school, Mark turned the corner. He regained his superior baseball skills. Grant knew it had happened when he could no longer move fast enough to get out of the way when Mark hit a ball back at him.

"I actually got hit by Mark a few times," Grant recalls. "He would say, 'Are you all right, dad?' and I would say, 'Not right now … maybe in a month.'"

It was also about this time when Mark realized that his friends were exploring new interests, and that maybe activities other than baseball could make him happy, could make his good life even better.

It was about this time he was hearing live music coming from behind garage doors around the neighborhood, and it sounded pretty good. Being part of a band sounded like a pretty good idea.

CHAPTER 5

Hearing the Beat of the Drum

Until he was in high school, Mark also played basketball. He was a normal kid who hung out with other kids who had other interests. When a couple of them started playing guitar, he decided that he wanted to be a musician, too.

"I was 13 or 14," Mark says. "I always liked listening to music and at some point I just got the idea that maybe I should learn how to play the drums."

His parents bought him a drum set, and Mark's love of music started to bloom. The first song he learned to play on the drums was "Island in the Sun" by the band Weezer. Mark doesn't know if they also bought ear plugs, but his parents always supported his musical interests, and those of his sister Michelle, who played the violin and piano.

"I'm very thankful my parents were into it because that's a noisy instrument," Mark says. "It's got to be somewhat of a nightmare."

"It seemed like a nice outlet ... a nice aggression outlet," his mom says.

Grant and Debbie Trumbo got home from work by 6 p.m. On the days he wasn't playing baseball after school, Mark practiced the drums with his friends.

Eventually, he also took up the guitar. He still plays both instruments well enough to jam with his friends in the music industry. One bonus of being a major league baseball star is that you cross paths with famous people in other walks of life. Maybe you've heard of some of Mark's music friends — Mike McCready, who is lead guitarist for the band Pearl Jam, and Ed King, guitarist and bassist for the Southern rock band Lynyrd Skynyrd.

"There are lots of musicians who are into baseball, and a lot of baseball players who are into music," Mark says. "I think it's fascinating to hear about their life on the road and our life on the road."

Once in a while, he's even helped out onstage, playing the drums in front of a big, music-loving crowd.

"It's kind of the same rush you get going out for a big at-bat at Yankee Stadium," Mark says.

Like performing musicians, performing athletes travel a lot, and although a lot of people envy them, as Mark notes, "You miss quite a few things that your friends are up to, and birthdays and holidays. That's kind of the trade-off."

So, does Mark envy the rock-and-roll lifestyle? His answer might surprise you, coming from a guy who does his job in front of 30,000 people every night.

"The music side of it, sure," he says, "but I've never felt comfortable in the spotlight. I really don't like any undue attention, ... on the field or outside the field. I get way more attention than I deserve."

Mark had been playing the drums for several years by the time he got to baseball's minor leagues, when he picked up a guitar for the first time, just for fun.

"I like learning new things," says the guy who always did well in school. "I just think it's a cool, creative outlet. I played some video games, too. ... It's cool, but I'd encourage kids to get outside.

"There's certainly more to life than baseball, but when you're a kid and that's already a large part of your identity, it isn't always easy to see that other activities can actually help make you a better baseball player."

Like basketball. Mark was always one of the taller kids on the block, and he was a big Los Angeles Lakers fan. He was built to play basketball, but he gave it up when baseball started to take up the whole year.

"I stopped right before I went into high school," he says.

Not too long ago, kids who were interested in sports often played more than one. These days, it's more common for even young kids to choose one, to specialize.

Although Mark always wanted to be a pitcher, he learned to play several positions during his Little League career, including catcher.

That started happening around the time Mark was in middle school.

"I think I was in the first generation that was really one-sport-only, year-round. I regret that I didn't at least try and play basketball and football."

Even though Mark thinks he might have missed something by specializing in baseball, he knows that it was the right path for him — it got him to the major leagues.

He also knows that he could have gotten hurt playing football, and that such an injury might have derailed his standout high school baseball career. But he believes that playing a lot of different games allows most kids to become better all-around athletes.

Mark spent a lot of time on the practice field with his dad, but it was never an excuse to fall behind on his school work. His parents made sure academics came first.

If Mark was certain when he was 8 that he would become a big league ballplayer, his parents were just as certain that he was not going to chase his dream without a backup plan.

"School was always extremely important," Mark says, and his parents expected him and Michelle to work to the best of their ability. "There was no slacking off."

In school, most subjects came easy to Mark. One did not.

"For me, math was always extremely difficult. It never made any sense," he says, even though he is the son of two engineers. That job demands very good math skills. But to Mark, math "always seemed like a foreign language … I think it taught me to scrap a little bit. It's a good life lesson. You've got to fight to get it done, even if it's super difficult."

For a hard-working, shy kid who was still getting a sense of who he was, working hard at both academics and athletics helped him keep a kind of balance.

"Sports was a huge part of what I did, and I think it can give you a lot of confidence if social situations aren't coming to you as easily," he reflects now, as a wiser adult. "Excelling in sports can be a nice way to get away from that a little bit."

CHAPTER 6

Heaven on the Mound at Angel Stadium

For a lot of kids, the jump from middle school to high school can be very scary. For a shy kid, it can be overwhelming. But Mark was a lucky shy kid — he had baseball, which helped him to fit in quickly.

He made the varsity team as a freshman. But for the first time, he wasn't the biggest and baddest player on the team. He was one of the new kids who had to spend a season watching and learning from the older players at Villa Park High.

"I think there were four or five of us who made the varsity team as freshmen," Mark remembers. "I rode the bench the entire season."

If he had joined the junior varsity team, Mark would

have played much more that year, but with the advice of his dad, he had always chosen to play at the highest possible level. Playing "up," they believed, was the best way to stay focused and improve quickly.

"I do feel it's best to surround yourself with better competition," Mark says. "So I was fine with that, and if I got an at-bat in a blowout, great."

Mark got very few of those at-bats, but that would change the following year.

He played very well in the summer league before his sophomore season, and people noticed. When he was 15, he got regular playing time at first and third base, and in the outfield, but remember — even though he had excellent fielding skills, Mark always thought he would be a big league pitcher.

That wasn't his main position in high school until one of his teammates got into trouble. That boy was the team's top pitcher, and one day, he got into an ugly argument with an umpire. He was suspended from the team, and Mark moved up in the pitching rotation. Because pitching is so hard on your arm, pitchers don't play every game — they alternate with other pitchers on the team.

After that, things happened in a hurry. In a matter of weeks, a 16-year-old kid was on the mound at Angel Stadium, warming up to pitch in the championship game of the CIF Southern Section. That's the sports organization for 585 high schools in Southern California, and its final tournament of the year is a very big deal.

The kid who had worked so hard since he was 6, who had stared at that mound every summer he could remember, now was standing on it. The kid who used to watch his favorite players hit home runs into the rock formation in center field now could feel it looming over his shoulder as he looked toward home plate to see what pitch the catcher was signaling him to throw.

It was 2002, and later that season, the Angels would go to the World Series. Mark felt like he was in the World Series already.

Mark led the Villa Park Spartans to the sectional title in the stadium where he would make his major league debut eight years later.

Mark's friends, Kurt Gottschling and Dane Ferguson, also were on that team. They had been playing together for nine years. Neither was surprised to see Mark dominate one of the best high school teams in California.

"Mark threw 95 [miles per hour] in high school," Kurt recalls. That's how fast the best major league pitchers throw. "He was beyond overpowering. He had control. He had command. He had good off-speed [slower] pitches. He made people look like idiots.

"When he was on the mound, every time he was out there he had a chance to throw a no-hitter."

A no-hitter means a pitcher played the whole game without the hitters on the other team having gotten on base, except by getting walked, hit by a pitch, or the catcher's interference.

For his impressive performance — on the mound *and* at the plate — Mark was named the CIF Player of the Year. Sophomores almost never get that honor, especially one who had little attention until the middle of the season.

"The guy was just a great two-way player," says Steve Fryer, who has covered high school sports for the Orange County Register newspaper for decades. By two-way, he means a player who is both a good hitter and a good pitcher, and it's almost unheard of in the major leagues.

That's why Babe Ruth is often called the greatest player in baseball history. He was a great pitcher *and* the best home run hitter of his era. Shohei Ohtani, who joined the Angels for the 2018 season, is the only MLB player in a very long time to play both ways.

Mark, says Fryer, "had a really nice, relaxed power swing. … Kind of a very mellow kid, but a heck of a competitor on the field. You knew he was special. He stood out. But you really didn't know if he would make it as a pitcher or a hitter. That decision was made for him, I think."

Remembering that season still brings a smile to Mark's face. It established him as a high-school star. His major league dream was starting to come into focus.

"I had some big hits," he says, modestly, "and started the final game at Angel Stadium. We ended up win-

In 2002, when the Villa Park High School Spartans won the Southern Section championship, Mark's earned run average (1.68) and his won-loss record (7-1) were the best on the team.

ning. One of my best friends got a bloop hit. That was really cool."

A "bloop" hit results from the batter changing his swing at the last second, or mistakenly making contact, but still running safely to first base when the ball drops between fielders.

Dane's blooper happened to be the game-winning hit in the title game, and more than 15 years later, Mark still teases him about it.

ROOKIE OF THE YEAR
Candidate
Mark Trumbo
Villa Park, CA

VILLA PARK, CA—"He had a fantastic year!"

That was Villa Park High Coach Tom Tereschuk's view of Mark Trumbo's sophomore season this year. The season was topped off by Trumbo being named the CIF Southern Section Division II Player of the Year.

Trumbo's hitting and pitching prove Tereschuk's statement.

He had a .391 average and led his team in hits (43), RBI (41) and home runs (7) in 31 games.

MARK TRUMBO

As a pitcher, the 6-4, 185-pound right-hander was 7-1 with an ERA of 1.68, team highs for the Division II champion.

What those impressive numbers don't show were the timeliness of many hits and pitching efforts.

Trumbo knocks Spartans into semifinal berth

VILLA PARK
In baseball:
Mark Trumbo did double duty for the Spartans as they defeated Woodbridge, 7-5, in the CIF-Southern Section Division II quarterfinals on May 24.

Trumbo broke a 5-5 tie with a two-run home run in the top of the seventh then came back in his second inning of relief and shut the Warriors down to record the victory.

The homer was his second of the week and seventh of the season.

"I was just looking for a good pitch to hit," he told the Daily

ter. "It's was my best cut of the game and I hit the ball hard."

The victory put the Spartans back in the semis for the second time in three seasons. The team won a CIF title in 2000.

"It was a fantastic job by Trumbo, but also a fantastic job by all of our guys in the lineup," Villa Park coach Tom Tereschuk said.

Woodbridge scored four times in the fourth to jump out to a 5-3 lead, but the Spartans responded with two in the top of the fifth to knot the score anew.

PREP NOTES

victory in the Spartans' 6-0 victory over Crescenta Valley on May 21. He had eight strikeouts in six-plus innings.

Ben Hanna was 1 for 1 with a double, sacrifice fly and two RBI.

In roller hockey:
The Spartans reached the quarterfinals before being knocked off by Arlington, 5-4, at Corona Inline.

CANYON

It was such a simple act that caused such total pandemonium.

Canyon's David Prager tapped a ball down over the net, causing it to bounce unchallenged on San Marcos' side. That was all it took to cause a mob of players, parents and Canyon students to swarm the floor at Cypress College on May 25.

Of course, who could blame them? With that tap down, Canyon sealed a 15-6, 8-15, 15-9, 15-13 victory over San Marcos - clinching the 2002 CIF-South-

volleyball title.

"It's awesome," coach Trent Jackson said after the match. "There are no words to describe how you feel when the hairs on the back of your neck are standing straight up and you're in that mosh pit, jumping up and down, and you've just won a CIF championship."

Canyon had the advantage from the beginning. Not just in the early lead and relatively easy 15-6 victory in the first game.

The Comanches also had a

He was only a sophomore, but Mark was named Player of the Year in his high school's division.

    The Villa Park coach that season was Tom Tereschuk, a no-nonsense guy whom Mark credits with helping him become a serious, no-nonsense player. "Coach T," however, remembers Mark as being just that when he arrived as a freshman at Villa Park.

    "He was a serious kid who worked very hard and was very focused — much more focused than you would

Members of the championship team included Mark, top row, fifth from the right, and his friends, Dane Ferguson, top row, third from the left, and Kurt Gottschling, bottom row, second from the right.

expect for a kid that age," Tereschuk says. "He wasn't just a baseball zombie. He was very good in school. It was expected that he was going to go to a four-year university. He was a very strong academic kid, but just a very serious, focused kid."

That season marked Mark's arrival as one of the top high school players in California. Soon, colleges wanted to recruit him, and scouts for professional teams began to track his progress. Kids like this are called "prospects." But Mark was only 16 — he had a lot of high school baseball left to play.

"We were good," Dane says, "but Mark ... was the

best player on the team for three years in a row."

Dane's right, but Mark has never been the kind of guy to say so. Maybe that's why he has so many lasting friendships from his days in Little League and at Villa Park High.

"He obviously knew he was good, but he wasn't going to tell the world," Dane says. "Everyone knew he was good. There wasn't any hiding his talent."

But no one's perfect, right?

Dane likes to remind his pal just how imperfect he was. When Mark remembers that he seldom went skateboarding with the other kids, Dane says it was because Mark didn't want anyone to see him fall off.

"That's the pot calling the kettle black," Mark says, laughing. "When we were in high school, Coach T used to yell the same thing at Dane all the time when he was in the outfield: 'Dane, athletes don't fall down!'"

Villa Park had a nationally recognized baseball program throughout Mark's high school career, and the school took part in several national preseason tournaments. During his senior year, he led the Spartans to a big trophy in the 2004 Toyo Tires National Classic, winning the championship game at Cal State Fullerton.

The national tournaments, generally held in March and April, showcase promising players and give pro scouts the chance to see a lot of them in the same place.

Mark also was the winning pitcher in the title game of the El Dorado National Classic. It, too, was held at

Fullerton's Titan Stadium, where his dad often took him as a kid to see the nationally ranked Titans. The team is still a major college baseball power.

"Out of our starting nine, I think every single guy [on the Villa Park team] went on to play college baseball at a pretty decent level," Kurt recalls. "I think we were ranked Number 2 or Number 3 in the country, and I will say with that much talent ... nobody was even close to Mark's talent level."

If Mark was ever tempted to take his talent for granted, someone was always there to keep him grounded: his dad. Grant could be a tough critic, even when Mark was drawing attention from professional scouts.

Mark remembers a very humbling experience that happened after his amazing sophomore season. That summer, in 2002, Mark was invited to a camp held at Stanford University in Northern California, where pro scouts would study every player.

Elite high school players from around the country were invited to compete against each other and be evaluated as a possible pro prospects. Mark participated, and felt that he did really well.

"I felt I had a strong showing and was one of the better players," he says. "About two weeks after returning home, I got the report card back from camp and received a D."

A *D*? For the guy who pitched his team into the title at the CIF Sectional tournament?

"Someone clearly didn't think too much of what they saw at the time."

It wasn't the last time Mark would face disappointment during his career, but it was the first time it shook his confidence. But instead of crumbling, Mark stared down the bad report the way he would stare down an opposing pitcher in a clutch at-bat.

CHAPTER 7

The Pros Take Aim

Major League Baseball has a massive scouting system to identify the best amateur players. "Amateur" means people who don't play for money. The MLB system monitors their progress in high school through college, so Mark's success during his sophomore year at Villa Park put him on their radar.

Before long, scouts from just about every major league team were tracking and sending back reports to the home office on this big kid who could throw a baseball through a wall, and hit one way, way over it.

Baseball scouts travel with two tools — a radar gun and a stopwatch. The radar gun measures the speed of pitches, and helps determine whether a young pitcher has a strong enough arm for the major leagues. The number on the gun that gets the most attention is the velocity of a fastball, but scouts also measure the speed and spin rate of the other pitches someone throws.

The stopwatch measures how long a pitcher takes to wind up and send the ball to home plate. That matters, because base runners are more likely to steal against pitchers who are slow to let go of the ball.

Scouts also use a stopwatch to measure the running speed of position players, timing how long it takes them to run from home plate to first base, and also from first base to third. A "position" player is any player other than the pitcher.

Most scouts weren't too interested in Mark's base-running ability. He had average speed for a big, powerful guy, and he was a smart base runner — he knew when and how far to lead off the base, when to try to steal, and how to run the bases when he wasn't the only base runner. But most scouts wanted to watch him on the days he was scheduled to pitch.

"That was what he was known for," Kurt says. "He was not actually known for hitting. He had massive power, but every scout around the country was there to see him pitch."

Not only was Mark's mid-90s fastball at the pro level, he also threw other kinds of pitches that fooled batters, and added to his value as a future professional. So a lot of the people sitting near home plate when he was pitching weren't just fans — they were pointing radar guns at him every time he wound up to throw.

That must have been a bit intimidating for Mark, who had to try to focus on the catcher's mitt with dozens of devices pointed at him that looked like "Star Trek" phasers.

Mark wasn't the only star pitcher in baseball-rich Orange County. Just a few miles away at Foothill High School in Santa Ana, future major leaguer Phil Hughes was also drawing a lot of attention from pro scouts.

After high school, Phil was snatched up by the New York Yankees, and emerged quickly as a top-flight player. Eventually, he pitched in the 2009 World Series, and the next year, he won 18 games. In Major League Baseball, pitchers who win 20 games are truly remarkable. If you win anything close to that, you're among the elite.

In high school, Phil and Mark were in the same grade, which meant that, sometimes, scouts had to work tight schedules on the days both boys pitched.

Mark's dad remembers one such day when Mark was pitching against a top team from Northern California.

"We were playing a team that came in from the San Francisco area to play Villa Park," Grant Trumbo says. "There were about 30 scouts who came to see Mark pitch. So, Mark pitched a couple of innings, and when he was done on the mound, they all got up and left, because Phil was pitching over at Foothill."

Mark and Phil developed a friendly rivalry during

Mark Trumbo

In Villa Park's biggest games, the senior showed that his best asset wasn't his arm or bat — it was his will to win.

Story by STEVE FRYER
Photo by NICK KOON
The Orange County Register

The will to win.

"We've all seen it, in different sports," Villa Park coach Scott Luke said. "We've seen that competitor who is not going to let his team lose. Mark has that."

Mark Trumbo's will to win, his ability to be that competitor who is not going to let his team lose, was as evident as ever when Villa Park played Temescal Canyon of Lake Elsinore in a CIF-Southern Section Division II first-round playoff game.

Trumbo hit a two-run home run in the first inning, then drove in Villa Park's other run, the winning run, in the bottom of the 16th inning in a 3-2 victory.

It was not the first time Trumbo took the Spartans to victory. He did it frequently and convincingly in an outstanding season that made him the Register's Orange County Baseball Player of the

"That was awesome," he said. "We were just playing flawlessly in that tournament."

He batted .425 and hit .741 with runners in scoring position. Trumbo slugged nine home runs, drove in 36 runs and scored 30. He had 37 hits in 29 games.

On the mound, the right-handed Trumbo, who is 6-foot-5 and 215 pounds, was 10-2 with a 2.20 ERA. He struck out 89 in 73⅓ innings.

One of his best pitching efforts came in Villa Park's first Century League game against Canyon, which was judged to be the Spartans' chief competition for the league championship. Trumbo pitched a two-hitter with 10 strikeouts and one walk.

Canyon coach Joe Hoggatt saw Trumbo possessed the will to win that early April game.

"The kid is extremely talented, obviously," Hoggatt said. "But the one thing I was most impressed by is that you could tell he was not going to lose that game."

As one of the best high school players in California, Mark got a lot of attention not only from the media, but from professional baseball scouts.

RETURN TIME: *Villa Park's Mark Trumbo is one of the nation's top prospects. Century League rivals Canyon and Villa Park begin the season atop Southland rankings.*
ROBERT LACHMAN *Los Angeles Times*

high school, and they competed against each other in the local summer leagues. They even competed while negotiating their first pro contracts. It turned out that Mark's offer was $25,000 more than Phil's. That's a lot of money, but not when you're signing a contract for more than $1 million.

Phil Hughes was not the only other future major leaguer making waves in Southern California when Mark was in high school. Brad Boxberger, who led the American League with 41 saves for the Tampa Bay Rays in 2015, was also pitching at Foothill High in 2004. (A "save" is awarded to the pitcher who comes in at the end of the game and holds the lead.)

The top prospect in the country was Matt Bush. He was a pitcher for Mission Bay High School in San Diego, about 80 miles south of Orange County. Eventually, he would play for his hometown professional team, the San Diego Padres, but in 2004, he pitched against Mark's Spartans in a tournament during their senior year.

"There were probably 75 or 100 scouts there," Dane says. "It seemed like every single seat was filled with scouts who came to watch those two guys. That was pretty cool. Every single radar gun was lighting up."

Both pitchers threw well that day, and Mark had a big hitting day, too. Even though he hit two doubles, and Villa Park won, 3-2, the scouts were more interested in Mark's arm than his bat.

During Mark's senior year, his dad was thinking about where Mark would play ball after he graduated. Grant had played baseball at the University of Southern California, and he hoped to steer his son toward that school if Mark did not sign a pro contract right after high school.

#2 Dane Ferguson • #12 Mike Vass • #32 Mark Trumbo (Varsity players all 4 years)

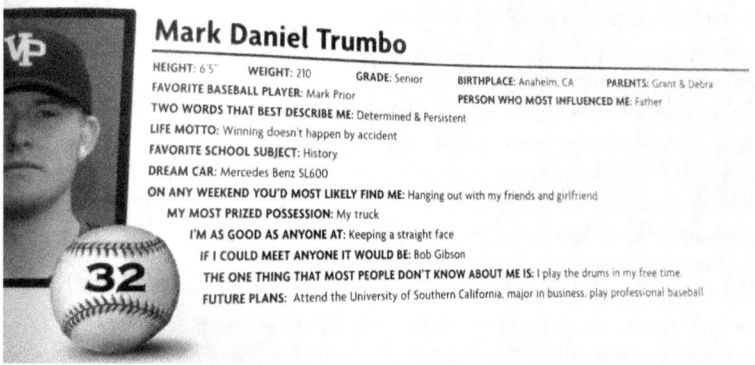

Mark Daniel Trumbo

HEIGHT: 6'3" **WEIGHT:** 210 **GRADE:** Senior **BIRTHPLACE:** Anaheim, CA **PARENTS:** Grant & Debra
FAVORITE BASEBALL PLAYER: Mark Prior **PERSON WHO MOST INFLUENCED ME:** Father
TWO WORDS THAT BEST DESCRIBE ME: Determined & Persistent
LIFE MOTTO: Winning doesn't happen by accident
FAVORITE SCHOOL SUBJECT: History
DREAM CAR: Mercedes Benz SL600
ON ANY WEEKEND YOU'D MOST LIKELY FIND ME: Hanging out with my friends and girlfriend
MY MOST PRIZED POSSESSION: My truck
I'M AS GOOD AS ANYONE AT: Keeping a straight face
IF I COULD MEET ANYONE IT WOULD BE: Bob Gibson
THE ONE THING THAT MOST PEOPLE DON'T KNOW ABOUT ME IS: I play the drums in my free time.
FUTURE PLANS: Attend the University of Southern California, major in business, play professional baseball

When Mark and Dane were seniors, the Villa Park baseball program told their stories.

He took Mark to a game between the Fullerton Titans and the USC Trojans at Titan Stadium. He introduced him to Mike Gillespie, who was head coach of USC. Sometime later, they all met at the university.

"I was extolling the virtues of what Mark had done, and promoting him as best I could," Grant says. "Mike

Mark is flanked by his parents, Grant and Debbie Trumbo.

Gillespie finally says, 'We know all about Mark. You don't have to add anything,' and essentially says, 'We're going to give him a full scholarship.'"

That's quite an honor — it means the school would pay for Mark's education, housing, and his expenses, for four years. To score that kind of support, you have not only superior baseball skills, but good character and good grades.

Still, Mark faced a tough decision — go to college, or go right into professional baseball, probably at a minor-league level. Should he make his dream come true right away, or spend more time improving, and turn pro a few years later at a higher level for more money?

Because teams need a lot of pitchers, those players, if they're any good, are always in demand.

When he met with scouts from various major league organizations, "virtually no team considered me as a position player," Mark says. "Neither did I."

CHAPTER 8

A Scholarship or a Paycheck?

Mark graduated from Villa Park High, and was a big-time prospect who could have been selected in the first round of Major League Baseball's amateur draft in June 2004. But he was chosen in the 18th round, and there's a story behind that.

First, it helps to understand what the draft is, and how it works. Other sports also use a draft process to select amateur players coming out of school, but the MLB draft is a bit different from, say, the NBA or NFL drafts. It's more common for baseball players to be drafted directly out of high school than for basketball or football players.

The actual draft is fairly simple. Each big league

HIGH SCHOOL BASEBALL

Trumbo nearing a major moment

The Villa Park ace has a scholarship to USC, but the pros will come calling this June.

By STEVE FRYER
THE ORANGE COUNTY REGISTER

Decisions, decisions. Fastball or curveball? USC or major-league baseball?

Whichever Villa Park pitcher Mark Trumbo chooses, the results likely will be excellent.

He signed with USC last fall, but his performance this season has enhanced another opportunity — he probably will be selected in the early rounds of the major-league draft in June.

"I've talked to a majority of the major-league teams," Trumbo said, "and a number of them have sent people to come to our house. If all goes well, I should be drafted pretty high up there."

How high is high enough to make him turn pro and eschew USC?

"I don't know," he said, "and it doesn't help any to speculate. Let's just say it would have to be a very good offer for me to not go to USC."

It long had been Trumbo's dream to attend and play baseball at USC. He visited during the summer, just a casual walk-around-the-campus visit that did not have the trappings of an official recruit-

SEE TRUMBO • PAGE 16

team may draft any high school senior or any college player who has finished his junior or senior year. The teams choose in reverse order of their won-loss record the previous season. So, that means the weaker teams get first shot to draft the players generally considered to be the best prospects. That's how other sports draft,

> **BaseBall America** NEWS **ESPN**
>
> ### Angels Land Trumbo For Record $1.425 Million
>
> By Jim Callis
> August 16, 2004
>
> It was widely known that Mark Trumbo wanted a seven-figure bonus to give up a baseball from the University of Southern California. And it's no secret that Angels owner Arte Moreno pockets and is willing to dig into them in order to improve his team.
>
> So when Trumbo signed for $1.425 million as an 18th-round pick on Saturday, setting a re non-draft-and-follow selected after the 10th round, it wasn't a surprise. But this was: Anah making him a full-time third baseman.
>
> When Baseball America ranked Trumbo, a product of Villa Park (Calif.) High, as the No. 31 the 2004 draft, it was as a righthanded pitcher. But the more the Angels scouted him this s more excited they got about tapping into his powerful bat on a full-time basis.
>
> "The last time he pitched, he threw 96 mph with 11 94s, so maybe we're crazy," Anaheim director Eddie Bane said. "We were going to send him out as a two-way guy when we draft
>
> "Then we thought about it, and the pitching will always be there if he doesn't make it as a l

The University of Southern California offered Mark a scholarship to play baseball, and the Angels offered him a professional contract worth almost $1.5 million.

too — worst teams get first chance to select the best new players.

Players who get drafted in the first round get the most money from the team that wants them. Remember Phil Hughes, Mark's rival from another high school in Orange County? He was a first-round draft choice in 2004. In 2009, Phil's younger high school teammate, Brad Boxberger, was also a first-round draft choice, but only after taking the other path — he played several years in college.

Here's how things get complicated.

Remember, the University of Southern California wanted Mark to play for the Trojans, and offered him a scholarship at one of the best college baseball programs in the country. Mark signed what's called a "letter of intent" to play at USC. Top-prospect high school players in other sports often sign such letters, which announce their intentions, but also allow them to decide later to sign with a pro team if they're selected in the draft, either out of high school or after their junior year in college.

By signing the letter with USC, Mark was signaling that he would choose to go to college if he wasn't drafted by a team he wanted to play for.

So, with the help of his parents and advisers, Mark was able to work out a deal with his hometown team — the Angels. The team could sign him for first-round money, but wait until the 18th round to draft him without worrying about other teams grabbing him. If another team did, he could go to school, and hope to play for the Angels later.

Mark was a good student, and he enjoyed many of the subjects he probably would have studied in college, but all his life he had wanted to play for the Angels at the stadium where he grew up watching them. Their offer — a signing bonus of $1.45 million — was first-round money. It was too good to refuse.

Mark's dad, Grant, and Eddie Bane, the Angels scouting director, worked on the deal for a long time. It wasn't finished until the week that Mark was supposed to move into the dormitory at USC.

Debbie Trumbo, Mark's mom, always knew what he wanted to do.

"I remember someone asking him if it was his dream to pitch at USC, and he said no," she remembers. "He said he would be happy to play at USC, but his dream was to be a major league ballplayer."

Even at 18, Mark understood that there was more to baseball than hitting or throwing a ball. It was a business, and he made a business decision. He might be playing a game, but suddenly, he wasn't a kid anymore.

"I remember what Mark said to me at that time," Grant says. "He said, 'Let's do it, because from a business standpoint you can't turn that down.'"

Hundreds of young, superior players have to make this decision every year, and there are strong arguments on both sides.

If you're a top prospect who signs right out of high school, you can secure your future with a big payday. Often, you never again have to worry about how to make a living. You also avoid the possibility of getting seriously injured playing in college, which can limit or end your baseball career.

But, if you go to college, you have at least three more years to mature. You continue to develop both your playing and thinking skills, while getting started on a good education that will be valuable if a baseball career doesn't work out. And for most players, it doesn't, at least not in the long term.

Because college players generally are more advanced, they spend less time in the minor leagues than players who get drafted out of high school. So, although younger draftees get a three-year head start, and are paid to play, usually they take longer to get through all the ranks of the minor leagues, and there are many, before they get to the big leagues.

The Angels scouted Mark as a pitcher, and drafted him with the idea of developing him into one of their starters. Mark was a big fan of right-hander John Lackey, who, as a rookie, won the seventh game of the World Series for the Angels in 2002.

"I always saw myself as a starting pitcher," Mark says. "John Lackey was a guy who was fun to watch. He was a bigger guy, and he threw like I did. He was probably a fair bit better than me, but it was at least somebody I could look at and say, 'This is a good guy to watch and learn from.'"

When he signed with the Angels, however, Mark had no idea that soon he would have to choose a different role model to help mold him into a major leaguer.

He had no idea that his lifelong dream of pitching in the major leagues was about to explode.

CHAPTER 9

A Crushing Blow

Mark couldn't wait to get to the minor leagues and show off his talented right arm to the Angels.

But first, he had to show it to the team doctor, Lewis Yocum, a highly respected arm and shoulder specialist.

Every player signed by a major league club — whether he is an 18-year-old prospect or a 30-year-old veteran — must undergo a complete physical exam before any contract is final.

No one, including Mark, had any reason to believe he wouldn't sail through his, and get a perfect health report.

Pitching puts a lot of strain on many different parts of the arm and shoulder, and pitchers commonly suffer a variety of problems. Mark had pitched for 10 years without any serious arm trouble. But maybe he had pitched too much, too young.

Today he recalls Dr. Yocum's exam. "He didn't like what he saw in my elbow," Mark says. "He said it was arthritic and showed 'signs of overuse.' That's a big deal."

Arthritis is a disorder of the joints. It often occurs with normal aging, but putting too much stress on a joint also can cause the problem. Sometimes, it takes a while before people with arthritis even know they have it. Arthritis can be treated, but it can't be cured. Overusing a joint, like pitching with an arthritic elbow, makes it painful, stiff, and swollen.

Mark was devastated. All of a sudden, a doctor's report about a problem he never knew he had turned his dream into a nightmare.

As Mark puts it, "It was just a gut punch. When he said, 'I don't think it's in the best interests of the Angels to sign this guy,' it was a brutal feeling."

His life, he says, "had come crashing down."

After the terrible news the doctor delivered, Mark and Grant drove home. Their disappointment hung like a black cloud inside the car. All the color had gone out of the world, and the future seemed dark dark dark. Like most clubs in such situations, the Angels would almost certainly pull out of the deal.

It took a while for the shock to wear off, but eventually Mark realized he had a college scholarship at USC to fall back on. "It was kind of like your dreams are crushed, but going and getting your education at a great school is not a bad thing," he says now.

His attitude, maybe, was shaped by the attitude Debbie Trumbo showed her son when she was ill. It almost certainly was shaped by all those years of hard work. Being really good at what you do, whether it's baseball or arithmetic, doesn't happen without learning from failure.

Mark's mom still marvels at how her son handled that disappointment. But, 14 years later, she nearly breaks into tears remembering when she got the call from the doctor's office.

"I was waiting and waiting, and finally Mark called and he said, 'Mom, they don't like something about my arm, so they're not going to sign me,'" Debbie Trumbo recalls.

"We had just talked to USC and told them Mark was signing with the Angels, and I had this image of the carriage pulling up to the castle, and it crumbling before he ever got out of it. I thought, Oh my God, is everything gone now?"

The Trumbos soon learned that all of the hard work *had* paid off, that everyone's hopes and dreams were still possible. The Angels were giving Mark a second chance.

Mark was supposed to meet with the Angels and sign his contract that same night, but he and his dad assumed the meeting was off because he failed his physical.

Mark showed up anyway.

He met with Scouting Director Eddie Bane, who told him that the team hadn't scouted him enough … as a *hitter*, and it was the team's fault.

Bane sent him to a batting workout with the Quakes. That was the Angels' low-level minor league team in Rancho Cucamonga, about an hour northeast of Orange County, and Bane wanted to see what Mark could do there as a hitter.

Days later, Mark was facing fastballs from a promising young pitcher. He sent them flying, his elbow in no way a problem at the plate. The Angels were impressed, and they set up a tryout for Mark at Angel Stadium.

A little more than two years after Angel Stadium had been the site of Mark's greatest athletic triumph as a 16-year-old CIF Championship pitcher, he was back on that field, hoping to redefine himself as a top-flight hitter.

Mark stood in the batting cage. The pressure was intense. All of the Angels' top executives were there.

Manager Mike Scioscia, who was a star catcher for the Los Angeles Dodgers during Mark's early childhood, peered through the netting. General Manager Bill Stoneman, Eddie Bane, and Special Assistant Ben Hines also watched closely as Mark took dozens of swings in the stadium where he had always hoped to play as a pro.

The huge rock formation behind the center field fence seemed like a mountain. Once in a while, major league sluggers bounce balls off those rocks for home runs, but hitting them just once would have been quite an achievement for a kid right out of high school.

Only the most powerful major league batters hit home runs into the rock formation at Angel Stadium. In his tryout for the team, 18-year-old Mark regularly sent them into the same place, more than 400 feet from home plate.

But those rocks were right in Mark's power zone. He pounded them with so many balls that Scioscia, who still manages the team, marvels about it today.

"Here is this kid, cranking balls into the rocks in center field, just like Vladimir Guerrero," Scioscia said recently, "and Vlad's in the Hall of Fame."

Seven years earlier, Mark was splashing Little League balls into Mrs. Christensen's swimming pool. Today, he was splashing big-league balls into the waterfall flowing over the rocks at Angel Stadium.

The Angels liked what they saw. They liked it so much they did what few teams in a similar situation do — they decided not to revise Mark's original offer.

They signed him for the same big bonus he was supposed to get as a pitcher.

"I was kind of stunned," Mark says, "but they said, 'You're going to hit now. ... and we've got to find you a position.'"

It was the beginning of a new chapter in Mark's young career, one in which he had to reinvent himself as a major league hitter.

"It was like, man, I've got to figure this thing out," he remembers. "I didn't really know how I would stack up against the best hitters. It was always just something I could do. It was totally natural ability."

He knew it would take a whole lot more than "natural ability" to get to the big leagues, and he hadn't even laced up his cleats at the lowest level of the Angels' minor league system.

"In my mind, hitting was an afterthought," Mark says. "… I felt my calling was on the mound. That was a pretty tough pill to swallow."

Mark was headed for the Angels' minor league training camp in Arizona. He didn't really have a position.

"I had tried playing third base in high school, and I wasn't very good," Mark admits. "I had played left field and first base. But pitching always took most of the pie. I just never envisioned myself doing anything else."

He was going to have to work very hard to claim a new position. But Mark, of course, knew how to work hard.

CHAPTER 10

Welcome to Utah

Thousands of good, young ballplayers begin their journey to major league baseball in some small town you probably never heard of.

In Mark's case, it was a place called Orem, Utah.

Every major league team has a farm system that includes four levels and at least six teams. There are two teams at the rookie, or lowest, level. Two teams at the Class A level. There is only one team at the Double-A level, and one at the Triple-A level, where some players have been to The Show, and been sent back down to wait for another chance, or to recover from an injury.

The Orem Owlz are in the Pioneer League, which was the higher of the two Angels' rookie teams at that time. The league schedule is shorter than the professional baseball season, which starts in April. Pioneer League teams begin their season in mid-June. It's the only minor league level with such a short season. The young players coming out of the draft generally start at the low or advanced rookie level before being promoted to a full-season team.

Big-league teams sign dozens of young players every year. Then they slowly weed out about the same number as they move up through the minor league ranks over the course of each season.

Mark would start at the advanced rookie level, but first, he had to be evaluated at the Angels' extended spring training complex in Arizona.

It's called "extended spring training," because the big-league players have left to start their season. Minor league players and injured major leaguers work out here until they join their teams.

Mark was on his own for the first time, and everything was so new that he almost missed his first professional practice. He had overlooked a change on the schedule, and left his hotel too late.

"I remember driving to the field and pulling into the parking lot when the entire team was less than five minutes away from our first practice," Mark says. "I somehow made it out onto the field, but I can't remember if my shoes were tied."

The lowest minor league levels focus on instruction. How you perform becomes increasingly important as

Even at the lowest minor league level, such as the Orem Owlz, where Mark started, "The worse player is probably one of the best players you ever played against," he says.

players progress from the rookie and full-season Class A teams to Double A and Triple A.

"The Pioneer League was a nice stepping stone for me because it was filled with college talent," Mark says. "I skipped the lowest level and was playing with and against kids that had three or more years of college training. It helped me grow up quickly."

"We played against really good competition in high school, but when you get to the pro ranks, it's the best of the best," Mark recalls. "The worst player there is probably one of the best players you ever played against."

The evaluation process never ends, and it doesn't always seem fair. Players who are selected highest in the draft, or given the biggest signing bonuses, get more chances to prove themselves, because teams have made a larger investment in them.

Because Mark received a large bonus, he didn't have much to worry about at first. But he knew, from all his work with his dad and his coaches, that the extra effort you make allows you to be your best when the games begin. Especially when you're proving yourself at a new position.

Everyone in the minors has natural ability, everyone is talented.

But, as Mark observes, "It's not that [their] tools are better. It's the consistency that's better. I played with some guys in the minor leagues with exceptional tools — some probably better than what you see in the majors. But they were not able to do it consistently. Those are the guys that just don't make it."

Even though he struggled with learning a new position and with living away from home, Mark enjoyed that summer in Orem. He was getting paid to play baseball. What could be better than that?

"There was wonderful scenery," he says about Utah. "The ballpark had a picturesque mountain range behind center field, and it was ... fun to go to the ballpark every day."

In 71 games that summer, Mark's batting average was .274. That number is simply the percentage of hits a batter gets out of all his at-bats, but it's expressed with three digits. If a player has 100 at-bats in a season, and gets 25 hits, his batting average is .250.

Mark had 10 homers, and 45 runs batted in (RBIs), a number that signals how good you are at getting a hit when your teammates are on base. Those are very good numbers for an 18-year-old playing such a short season. His terrific power was showing up much earlier than an average first-year player, who seldom hits home runs. He seemed to be on his way, but tough challenges lay ahead.

CHAPTER 11

Back to Baseball School

There's a lot more to baseball than just throwing and catching a ball, hitting it with a stick, and running around the diamond. It's a very complex sport, and the best players are the best thinkers, because there's a lot to consider in just about every situation a batter, pitcher, or fielder faces.

Every level, from Little League to the major leagues, has a learning curve.

When Mark was a kid, he could hit the ball farther than anyone else. He could throw it harder. In high school, all those hours of practice with his dad paid off, but even after graduation, he still was a bundle of raw talent waiting to be formed.

"Whether you're a high school player or even higher

than that, it's important to be honest with yourself," Mark says. "If you think too highly of yourself and you're not honest with yourself in certain areas, you may not put in the work needed to improve."

Mark always had the benefit of good coaches, who insisted on a strong work ethic. That means committing yourself to doing the work it takes to excel, even on the days you don't feel like it. There's a saying in baseball that defines a strong work ethic: "The harder I work, the luckier I get."

When you sign a pro contract and start getting a paycheck to play baseball, the work gets harder. Coaches get tougher. Your ability to learn is the biggest key to your future.

The first professional coach to give Mark the tough love that would make him a better player was Craig Grebeck. He was a minor league instructor at the Arizona camp, and a former major league infielder.

Craig might have been tough on Mark because he himself had learned the hard way what it meant to be tough. He hit his first major league home run off of Nolan Ryan, a hard-throwing, Hall of Fame pitcher. In Craig's next at-bat, Ryan hit him hard in the chest, and broke his rib.

Craig wasted no time getting into Mark's head during those early weeks in the Angels' camp in Arizona.

One day, Craig pulled him aside and told him that he didn't have a major league swing. That he better develop one, or he wouldn't be around very long.

"Hey Bub," Mark remembers him saying, "you might think you're going to be around forever, but if you don't start making some adjustments and get your act together, they can get rid of you like they get rid of everyone else."

To someone who had always been able to hit the ball a ton, the remark stung. But Mark still heard the message behind it, loud and clear.

"Sometimes you need a little bit of fire lit under you."

Mark went to work with Craig. He also went back to a strategy that had always helped him improve. He picked out a successful player who had a body type similar to his, and tried to copy that guy's swing.

The player he chose was six-time All-Star Paul Konerko. Like Mark, he was tall and powerful. A first baseman, he played 18 seasons in the major leagues, most of them with the Chicago White Sox. When Mark was learning a "major league swing," Konerko was in the prime of a career in which he hit 439 home runs.

"I've always learned best by watching someone do it, and then trying to copy it," Mark says. "If I can see it, I can mimic it, so I started watching Paul Konerko hit."

"That's some of the best advice I can give younger players," Mark says, "to find someone who really does it the right way and try to copy [his] moves, if you can."

Mark advises youngsters to copy someone who looks

like them. "If you're a tall, lanky guy, it's not good to watch a short, squatty guy. It's going to be hard to do that."

Craig Grebeck was just the first coach or manager to help shape and direct Mark's minor league career. Others would help him refine his swing, and understand the basics of playing first base. They would help him realize that there's only one way to play baseball — the right way.

The manager at Orem was another no-nonsense guy. Tom Kotchman made Mark play right. He figured that out the day he got thrown out at third base trying to steal.

Tom Kotchman, the manager of the Orem Owlz, was more impressed with Mark's hitting skills than his base-running decisions.

Most players try to steal a base only after the third base coach gives them a sign — in other words, they get permission to steal. But some players have what's called a "green light" to steal bases whenever they want. Those players not only have exceptional speed, but the smarts to understand when the time is right. Mark is the first to admit that he does not have exceptional speed. But that time, he thought he *was* fast enough, that the situation was a good one to try to steal, and that he didn't need a coach to tell him so.

He was wrong. He was out!

Manager Kotchman yanked him out of the game, and gave him an earful.

"That was the last time I attempted to put my blazing speed into use without permission," Mark notes, making fun of himself.

Today, Tom Kotchman scouts and manages at the rookie level for the Boston Red Sox. He remembers Mark the same way a lot of people do who watched him during those minor league years — that Mark didn't say much, but he made a loud noise every time he connected at home plate.

Theodore Roosevelt was president of the U.S. early in the 20th century. He was a robust man known for physical feats and bluster. He was famous for his policy: "Speak softly and carry a big stick," meaning that the U.S. should have a lot of power, but not bully anyone. The way Mark plays baseball fits that description, and it has since he first stepped up to a batting tee.

"With [Mark]," Tom says, "the power was the real intriguing thing. The ball carries well in the Pioneer League, but some of the balls he hit, they aren't supposed to fly that far."

They flew so far that Tom tells a story that reminds

you of Mark's buddies talking about the Christensens' pool.

Every time Mark took batting practice at Orem, it was "must-see TV." People gathered around the field were amazed that he could hit the ball so far that it sailed over a hill behind the fence in left center field.

"On the other side of the hill was this pond — probably about 425 feet away," Tom recalls. "They called it 'Lake Trumbo,' because that's where the balls he hit in batting practice would land.

"I didn't know it was called that until a year or two later, when [a team executive] said, 'Yeah, that's Lake Trumbo. People think that they can hit it there, but there's only one person that could.'"

Tom chuckled when he heard the story about Craig Grebeck's opinion of Mark's swing. Craig, who was 8 inches shorter and probably 60 pounds lighter than Mark, hit only 19 home runs during his 12-year major league career.

Tom imagines what their conversation was like. "You've got one guy that's really short and one guy that's really tall. ... I would like to have [seen] Craig Grebeck telling this giant that he doesn't have a clue."

The first season at Orem went pretty well, but Mark was still getting by on his natural ability. And he knew that although it would buy him some time, eventually it wouldn't be enough.

"I had no idea what I was doing," Mark says, "but because I got a little bit of money out of the draft, I probably had a little bit longer leash."

The Angels had a lot of good coaches to help him, but one in particular was going to tug on that leash until Mark was a lot farther along the path to the major leagues.

Rob Picciolo was a former major league infielder. Where he went to college and how he pronounced his last name led to his nickname — "The Pepperdine Peach."

Rob was a star at Pepperdine University in Southern California. He played nine seasons in the big leagues, but he didn't get there because of his bat. He was a skilled defensive player for three different teams. His career batting average of .234 and 17 home runs were unremarkable. He wasn't at all like Mark in other ways as well.

Rob was a tall, slender middle infielder, and Mark was a big, strong first baseman. That might have mattered if Rob was a hitting instructor. He played the positions a lot of smaller players do — second base, third base, and shortstop. But his job was to refine Mark's defensive skills at his new position, first base.

That process covered almost all of Mark's minor league career.

Mark needed to move quicker, and improve his footwork. First basemen must be able to field the ball thrown by a teammate from almost any other part of the infield, and they have to do it in time to get the runner out. So the

Rob Picciolo coached Mark for many years through the minor leagues, and even after he was called up to the big leagues, top. The coach was important in the Angels' system of player development. Mark says "Peach" made him a much better defensive player.

first baseman must have both the ball and his foot on the base before the runner touches it.

He also must catch ground balls and high fly balls all around the base.

"I had to do an immense amount of work, and Rob always was on me about that," Mark says. "We had this practice ball that bounced every different way, and for years part of almost every day's work was … to chase that ball. It improves your footwork and hand-eye coordination."

Hand-eye coordination is how well your hands respond to what your eyes see. For example, a hitter must time his swing according to how he reads the ball leaving the pitcher's hand.

Rob clearly saw something special in Mark, because he never gave up on him. No amount of drills or practice was enough, and there were times Mark got tired of them.

"It's hard, because at the time you're a little resistant to go out and do all those extra things," Mark says. "I think that's just natural. When you're younger, you question, why are we doing this?

"Then, as you get a little bit older, you realize the coaches aren't making you do it because it doesn't matter."

Rob kept grinding away, and Mark kept improving. It would be years before he fully appreciated the impact that "Peach" had on his career. If any one person was responsible for Mark becoming a big league first baseman, it was Rob Picciolo.

When Mark was 31, Rob passed away. It was unexpected, and a very sad day for Mark. Rob was critical to Mark's success as a defensive player, but not long after Rob died, Mark said he might have benefited from Rob's help when he was struggling at the plate, too.

"I think guys who have some sympathy for how hard this game is make the best instructors," Mark says. "I think Peach was excellent."

CHAPTER 12

Figuring Out Failure

Very few successful people are strangers to failure. The best hitters in Major League Baseball fail almost 70% of the time.

They strike out. They hit fly balls. They are called out running to first base on ground balls. So there are a lot of ways to fail as a hitter. Even the greatest stars in the sport go through frustrating slumps, and wonder if they'll ever get another big hit.

If you ask Mark if he ever wanted to give up and go home during the five seasons he spent in the minor leagues — or even during his major league career — you might be surprised at the answer.

"Probably too many times to count, if we're being honest," Mark says. "Even during my best seasons, there come times when things seem so bleak that quitting seems like it might be a huge relief."

Mark came out of his first full minor league season feeling pretty good. He was moving up in the system, but the next year he wondered if he would ever be good enough to play first base at Angel Stadium.

"The 2006 season was my worst professional season by far," Mark recalls.

He was assigned to the Cedar Rapids Kernels, a full-season Class A team in Iowa. The talent level wasn't too much higher than at Orem. The comfort level was another story.

"Playing in a place as foreign to me as Iowa proved to be a challenge," Mark says.

He felt more at home in Utah because even though Orem was smaller, it felt more like his hometown in Southern California. It was scenic. The summertime weather was similar. The people out West were more easygoing.

Iowa is where Mark met Hank Conger, a catcher who would become a very close friend as they climbed through the Angels' minor league system together. Not much else about the place felt good. The weather in the Midwest was unpredictable. It was just *different.*

In addition, Mark says, "The problems with my swing were exposed at the higher level."

He batted just .220 that summer. In the low minor leagues, .250 or so might be an acceptable batting average, but hitters at all levels of baseball try to hit .300.

In 2008, Mark had a good season at Class A Rancho Cucamonga, where he swung a big bat and refined his fielding skills.

It was his lowest batting average at any level, from Little League to the majors, and it shook his confidence.

It would not be the last time. Mark's numbers improved the next season, also in Iowa, and in 2008, he moved back to California and had a big power season at Class A Rancho Cucamonga.

Mark's 2009 season at Double-A Arkansas would be a major turning point in his career. But at first, it looked like a major turn in the wrong direction.

"I was hitting .200 or .215 at the halfway point, and I just came off a season when I did quite well," Mark says. "I remember talking to some buddies and they were telling me you just have to try to enjoy yourself, and I was like 'Yeah, but this is brutal. I'm not doing *anything*.'"

As a member of the Triple-A Salt Lake City Bees, Mark was back in the West, where he felt more comfortable, and was playing in the highly competitive Pacific Coast League.

Mark figured it out. He realized that the ballpark in the city of Little Rock was too big to spend the whole summer swinging for the fence. So he stopped swinging so hard, and concentrated on hitting singles and doubles instead of home runs. The result showed up in his batting average — he finished the season batting .291. Batting average, of course, shows only how many safe hits a player has — it says nothing about the *kind* of hit, whether it's a homer or a single.

The next year, he was back in Utah, but at a much higher level. He was promoted to the Triple-A Salt Lake City Bees in the Pacific Coast League, where he proved that he belonged in the major leagues.

"It's a pretty big deal to come that far back when you're at .200," Mark says. "I proved to myself I could do it. If I get into a hole, I can figure it out."

Bobby Magallanes, the manager of the Arkansas Travelers, made sure Mark knew the value of his problem-solving skill.

"You need to remember this," Bobby told him, "and use it to your advantage in the future."

Mark never forgot the two extremes of that season. Still, as a major leaguer, he remembers the lesson learned:

If you find yourself in a hole, stop digging.

"When you get to this level, you have to have confidence," Mark says. "You've got to have some armor."

But before Mark headed to Salt Lake City, before he delivered a commanding performance at the highest minor league level, he faced one more crisis of confidence.

Playing a season of winter ball in the Dominican Republic in 2009 made him question if he was on the right path to the major leagues.

CHAPTER 13

A Detour to the Dominican Republic

It had been almost five years since Dr. Yocum told Mark that his arm was damaged, and that he had no future pitching in the major leagues. It had been almost five years since the worst day of his life. But Mark had found a way around the mountain that stood between him and his dream of becoming the best hitter he could be. That was that.

Or was it?

The ups and downs at the plate weighed on him even as he rose through the Angels' system to emerge as one of the top power-hitting prospects in the minor leagues.

In a 2008 season split between the A and AA minor league levels, Mark hit 32 home runs. But in the first half of his full season at Double-A Arkansas in 2009, he struggled before coming back strong to reach a batting average of nearly .300. Filled with the confidence that came with overcoming failure, Mark didn't want to sit out the long off-season. He wanted to play. To improve.

The Dominican Republic is a nation on the island of Hispaniola in the Caribbean Sea. It's famous for its high level of baseball, and many major league players come from the D.R. Because of its warm climate year-round, a lot of U.S. ballplayers go there during the off-season to play winter ball. In 2009, Mark was one of them.

This time, being so far from home wasn't the problem. This time, the problem was Mark.

"I barely lasted three weeks in winter ball," he remembers. "There were many fans happy to see me packing my bags. I played terribly."

So terribly, it seems, that Mark wondered if he was cut out to be a hitter. He wondered if it was time to restart his career as a pitcher.

Pitching was his thing. Pitchers were in total control of the game. On the mound, they stand 10 inches taller than everyone else on the field. Hitters have to look up to them.

Mark, who was 23 years old in 2009, didn't want to get stuck in the minor leagues. He knew guys who were 30 and still trying to make it to the big leagues, guys with no other career options. Mark thought there was something sad about that. Mark wanted to make the major leagues by the time he was 24, or go back to school, get a degree, and get on with his life.

"I just didn't want to be a guy who held on forever," he says.

But, suddenly, the guy who was so smart seemed to have lost his mind.

Switching back to pitching didn't make sense. It would mean Mark would have to spend more time in the minor leagues. And would his arm even work right? Sure, he'd done poorly in winter ball, but for three steps forward, sometimes you take a step back. Mark just couldn't see what everybody else could.

"Even after playing well in Double A, I didn't get the kind of feedback that made me think I was on the fast track to being a major leaguer," Mark says, to explain what he was thinking. "Pitching was something that came far more naturally to me, and I felt like that would be my best chance to fulfill my dreams."

So, Mark called his agent and told him that he planned to give up on being a big-league slugger to go back to mound. The next step would be to tell the Angels, and there was no guarantee they would welcome the news.

Mark knew he was about to make a decision that, someday, he would look back on as the one that helped him reach the majors, or the one that sent him back to school and to another career. So he did something smart.

He took a breath.

He counted to 10.

He slept on it.

Ancient advice says, "He who hesitates is lost," but, often, it's bad advice. There is a time for quick decision, and there is a time for careful deliberation.

"For whatever reason, I got a gut feeling that I needed to give hitting one more shot before making that call," Mark says.

He had listened to all the coaches who worked with him to improve his batting. He had made a lot of progress, but something was still holding him back.

He realized what was holding him back was himself. It was time to take more responsibility to make a future as a hitter.

"One of the biggest hurdles for any baseball player is trying to be respectful and accepting of coaching," he says, "but [also] understanding that not all of the information taught will apply to you."

Not too many major league players are as big as Mark, who is 6 feet, 4 inches tall. He felt that the swing his coaches taught didn't fit his body type. So he tried other ways to improve his skill.

Good timing.

CHAPTER 14

On Wings of an Angel

It's the moment every minor league ballplayer thinks about from the day he signs his first pro contract.

It might happen in the clubhouse after a game. It might happen while teammates board the bus to go home after a road series. It might even happen in the dugout during the fourth inning of a game.

The call comes from the big league club, and the manager pulls the player aside and tells him to pack up his stuff.

He's going to The Show.

Mark had wondered many times since third grade if the call would ever come. If not now, when?

He had absolutely dominated Triple-A baseball that

summer, batting .301 with 36 homers and 122 RBIs for Salt Lake City. He led the Pacific Coast League in homers, RBIs, and runs scored (103). He was named the season's top Triple-A power hitter. Not just for the PCL, but for all minor leagues in the whole country.

Being called up at the end of the season is an opportunity for major league coaches and managers to see how some of their top young players perform in a big-league environment. It's also a reward for having a strong minor league season.

In early September, after the Bees played a day game, the manager called Mark into his office. It was the part of the season when major league teams are allowed to expand their 25-man rosters before the playoffs. The Angels were expanding. And they wanted Mark.

Even better, they also wanted Hank.

Mark remembers Sept. 2, 2010, as if it were yesterday. "I found myself following my good friend Hank Conger and his dad on the drive back from Salt Lake City to Anaheim."

They drove 10 hours straight. Nobody complained about the distance. Finally, Mark was going to put on an Angels' uniform, and make his big-league debut in front of everyone who was important to him.

Getting the call didn't mean that Mark would get to play much. He sat on the bench for nine days before getting his first at-bat. He laughs about it now. "It happened in the blink of an eye," Mark remembers.

"It was 'Hey, you're up.' Hank was right in front of me. He struck out."

The pitcher was Jamey Wright. Mark had faced him in a minor league game early in the summer, and had hammered a game-winning, 3-run home run. This time, the pitcher was familiar, but the stage was sooo big.

Mark took his stance at home plate. He could barely breathe.

He watched the first pitch sail past, smack into the catcher's mitt.

Strike one.

He watched the second pitch sail past and disappear into the catcher's mitt.

Strike two.

On the next pitch, he swung, got a piece of the ball, and fouled it out of play.

He swung at the next pitch, too. He missed.

Strike three.

"I had thought about that moment for as long as I can remember," Mark says. "I know now that I wasn't in any frame of mind to have success. I would have swung at the rosin bag if he had thrown it."

He might have had more success if he *had* swung at the rosin bag, a small sack pitchers have at the back of the mound to rub and keep their hands dry

Mark didn't get his first major league hit until the final day of the season, three weeks later. He went hitless in his first 14 MLB at-bats, while his family came

Catcher Hank Conger worked his way through the Angels' minor leagues at the same time as Mark. The good friends were thrilled to be called up to The Show on the same day.

to every home game, hoping to cheer every time he was up.

"It was one of those funny things," Mark recalls, "where your parents come to the games and come to the games and after 15 or so games …"

So Grant and Debbie Trumbo weren't there when the wait ended Oct. 3 in Mark's last at-bat of the year. The Angels were playing the Texas Rangers at The Ballpark in Arlington on the last day of the season. Mark saw seven pitches from right-hander Mark Lowe before hitting the eighth safely into center field. His 2-run single broke open a tight game.

Rookies always are given the baseball after their first MLB hit. Mark's is displayed prominently in the living room of his parents' home in Orange County.

Mark had every reason to believe it would be the first of hundreds, maybe thousands, of hits he would record in the major leagues. Still, he was relieved.

"I was glad to get one hit, because who knows?" he says.

Getting called up at the end of the season did not guarantee that Mark would make the big-league club in 2011. But he was the top 2010 power hitter in the minor leagues, and had nothing left to prove at that level.

His time had come.

CHAPTER 15

The Show Stoppers

Any big-league player will tell you that it's tough to get to the majors, but it's even tougher to stay there.

It took more than five years for Mark to work his way up through the Angels' minor league system, but after spring training in 2011, he made the club and never looked back.

He got hits in eight of his first 10 games, starting every day at first base. He clocked his first big-league home run on April 12 in a 2-0 victory over the Cleveland Indians.

There would be hundreds more "Trumbombs," but no big-league player ever forgets the first one.

Mark's first really big game at the plate came a week later in Texas, where he had gotten his first big-league

It didn't take long for Mark to become popular among Angels' fans. He got eight hits in his first 10 games in 2011, and always took time to recognize the people who came to watch him play.

hit on the last day of the 2010 season. This time, he homered and drove in four runs in a 15-4 blowout victory. That win was even sweeter, because Mark, along with his close friends Hank Conger and outfielder Peter Bourjos, drove in nine of those 15 runs.

Not bad for the young guys batting at the bottom of the lineup.

Then came the gloom of June. Mark had a soft month, driving in just seven runs. But mostly, his rookie year was marked by his consistency.

In each of the other five months of the season, he drove in at least 13 runs, and finished with 29 homers and 87 RBIs. Those numbers were impressive enough for the Baseball Writers Association of America to give him the most votes of any position player as American League Rookie of the Year. He finished second overall, to pitcher Jeremy Hellickson of Tampa Bay.

If Mark's plan was to play first base on his hometown team for his entire career, he certainly was off to a great start. The local kid had made good. The future was bright, but the future is never certain.

Only three weeks after the Rookie of the Year vote, the Angels threw Mark a big curve.

They signed Albert Pujols, a future Hall of Fame first baseman, to a 10-year, $254 million contract. Mark had gotten comfortable playing that position, so, once again, he had to carve out a new role somewhere else on the field. Albert was a three-time National League Most Valuable Player — clearly, he was going to get almost all the playing time at first base.

"I think I was really happy in the sense that we got one of the best players in the game," Mark recalls. "I was thrilled that I would get to be teammates with a surefire Hall of Famer. But, at the same time, I was very unsure about what that meant for me."

Like most people, baseball players like to settle into a comfort zone. They like to know where they're going to play every day, and they like to know where they're going to bat in the lineup.

Mark didn't know any of that in 2012 when he started his second big league season. He would have to rely on everything he learned in the minors about how to accept change and make adjustments.

He started the 2012 season playing third base. That experiment didn't last very long. The Angels moved him to the outfield. By the end of the season, he had played 97 games in the outfield, 21 games at first base, and 23 games as the designated hitter (DH).

The designated hitter position has been used in the American League since the 1970s. It was adopted so that pitchers don't have to hit. The DH stays in the dugout when his team is playing defense, and bats for the pitcher. The National League doesn't use designated hitters — pitchers bat for themselves.

For most of the year, Mark was paired in the outfield with the Angels' new promising superstar — center fielder Mike Trout, who was voted Rookie of the Year in 2012. He would be voted the league's Most Valuable Player twice in his first five big league seasons. When this book was written during the 2018 baseball season, Trout still played center field for the Angels, and was at or near the top of the list of MLB home run leaders.

Trumbo and Trout — T and T — were quite a combination right from the start. Mark hit 32 homers in 2012, and Mike hit 30. Albert Pujols also hit 30, and the Angels finished with their biggest win total (89) in four years. But it was a tough division, and they didn't make the playoffs.

Mike arrived from the minor leagues a month after the season began. He quickly moved into the leadoff spot — the first guy in the batting order. Albert batted third, and Mark batted either fourth or fifth. The three spots in the middle of the lineup are called run-production slots, and that's where teams put their power hitters.

In his second full year as an Angel, Mark was joined on the team by rookie sensation Mike Trout. Their powerful hitting earned them the shared nickname "T and T." Here, as a Baltimore Oriole, Mark greets Mike in 2018, when the teams played a series at Angel Stadium.

The leadoff man's job is to get on base ahead of the big boppers, so they can score him with a hit or home run. If the leadoff hitter is also a power hitter, sometimes pitchers walk him to keep him from hitting a homer. But they can't use that strategy if the next hitter — and the one after him — also hits home runs. It's too risky.

In 2012, the Angels had another terrific hitter, Torii Hunter, who often hit second, between Mike Trout and the run-producers. Opposing pitchers had nowhere to hide.

With all those great hitters behind him, Mike had one of the best all-round rookie seasons in history. He batted .326, and led the major leagues with 129 runs and 49 stolen bases. And he didn't even play the full season!

A future Hall of Fame player, Albert Pujols, also joined the team in 2012, adding his big bat to the Angels' lineup. Before the game against the Orioles, he shares a laugh with Mark.

In 2013, Mike and Mark both took another step forward. Mike batted .323, with 27 home runs and 95 RBIs. He was second in the MVP vote, even though the

Angels finished with a losing record for the first time in five seasons.

Mark had his best offensive season yet, hitting 34 homers, and driving in 100 runs. He also played a lot at first base, because Albert had a foot injury that ended his season in July.

Here's what Mark's first full years in major league baseball looked like: As a rookie, he was the runner-up for Rookie of the Year in the American League. He improved both his home run and RBI totals in each of the next two seasons. He was half of the best pair of young sluggers in either league, and he was moving into the prime of his career.

Mark was playing for his hometown team, he was one of MLB's brightest young stars, he had every reason to believe he would have a long and productive career with the Angels.

He was wrong.

CHAPTER 16

Leading With His Heart

Mark arrived in the major leagues at a turning point for the Angels. The team had won its first World Series in 2002, and had reached the playoffs five of the next eight years. But in 2010, the Angels were coming off their first losing season in a long time.

With their new stars, Mark Trumbo and Mike Trout, they bounced back to have solid winning seasons in 2011 and 2012. But their pitching was not strong enough to get them back into the playoffs, and they stumbled backward in 2013.

The slide had little to do with Mark's performance. Albert Pujols was injured for much of the year, and

Angels' executives had just made one of the biggest mistakes in their history. They gave outfielder Josh Hamilton a contract that was too big, and it left them little money to pay for better pitching.

General Manager Jerry DiPoto decided that the best way to fix the pitching problem was to trade one of the team's top young players. With Albert under contract to play first base for eight more years, and Mike emerging as one of the best players ever, Mark was the guy.

"They [Mark and Mike] were two young players that we were obviously very excited about," says Angels' Manager Mike Scioscia. "I think we were all sorry to see Mark go, not only because of the talent, but because Mark was such a terrific young man."

Mike was surprised. He, like Mark, thought they would be together in the Angels lineup for a long time.

"I did," Mike says. "Mark's one of my good friends. I got called up, and he was up here. Obviously, he can hit for power and everything, but he's just a great guy."

In just three seasons, Mark had proved himself as one of the league's best power hitters, but he had been displaced at first base, and the Angels had plenty of power in their batting order.

If they had known that a couple of young pitchers who had come up through their minor league system, Garrett Richards and Matt Shoemaker, would have breakout seasons and help lead the Angels back to the playoffs in 2014, Mark might still be in Anaheim.

Instead, when DiPoto traded him to the Arizona Diamondbacks in December 2013 for two other young pitchers, Mark was heartbroken. But not surprised. Rumors had been swirling that one of the Angels' young sluggers — either Mark or Howie Kendrick — had to go.

"I had an idea this was serious," Mark told Bill Dwyre, a columnist for the Los Angeles Times, soon after the deal. "I kept hearing the rumors …"

He also told The Times, "I have deep roots here. I've been a lifelong Angels fan, and in many ways, it has been pretty much all I've known. It'll be a little tough."

He spent his childhood imagining himself as an Angel. He proved his skill in high school, and spent 5½ years working his way through the Angels' farm system. He averaged 32 home runs and 94 RBIs in his first three major league seasons.

What else does a guy have to do to keep his dream job?

Mark did what he has always done. He turned the page, and faced the next big challenge in a career that has been full of them.

"At some point, you have got to say, 'All right, this is my new role. This is where I'm at. You're no longer an Angel.' It took a while."

But before he moved on, Mark had some unfinished

Even though Mark had been traded to the Arizona Diamondbacks after the 2013 season, he still served as a host that year for the Angels' annual holiday party for kids.

business in Anaheim. Every year, he had served as a host at the Angels' Christmas party for underprivileged kids, but in 2013, he had been traded just days before the party. What happened next reminded the Angels of the kind of man they would soon be missing.

He called up the Angels, and asked if he could still come to the party.

"It blew us away," Manager Mike Scioscia says. "Here's a guy who was just traded to Arizona, and still wanted to fulfill an obligation, and see some underprivileged kids at Christmas. I think that says a lot about Mark."

People who knew Mark since he was little weren't surprised by his big heart. Brandi Aarvig, his third-grade teacher, certainly wasn't.

A couple of years earlier, just after Mark was called up to the major leagues, Ms. Aarvig, was still teaching at a nearby elementary school. But she was having a rough time. Nearly 20 years after watching Mark deal with the scary report of his mom's breast cancer, Ms. Aarvig was facing the same terrifying disease.

She was days away from having major surgery, and one morning, she wanted to stay home. But, Ms. Aarvig remembers, "Something told me to go to work that day."

So she did.

She and her students were in the computer lab when the principal called her and asked her to return to the classroom for a moment. Ms. Aarvig hesitated — she didn't want to leave her students alone in the lab.

"I quickly hurried over to my classroom," she recalls, because the principal sounded like there was an emergency.

There wasn't. The principal was making up a drama to hide a surprise.

"It was so weird," Ms. Aarvig says. "I peeked into my classroom and saw all the reporters, and my parents and daughter. I was shocked."

Her family members were all dressed in Angels' jerseys. Ms. Aarvig walked into the classroom. Mark was sitting in the corner, in her favorite chair, wearing his Angels' jersey.

He stood up, and Ms. Aarvig raced across the room to give him a big hug.

Angels' Manager Mike Scioscia, here with Mark before the game against the Orioles, remembers Mark not only as a good teammate, but as a kind and generous person.

"What are you doing here?" she asked.

"Somebody ... told me what was happening next week [her surgery], and I had to be here for you."

Ms. Aarvig still chokes up when she talks about that day. She had never forgotten Mark, and had followed his career through high school, the minor leagues, and the terrific rookie season he had just completed with the Angels. She admits to being the world's biggest Mark Trumbo fan. Then, and now.

"I was going through a very dark moment — that particular time in my life — and that morning I almost didn't go to work, because I was having a hard time living," she says, tears welling up. "I went to work, and there he was. I have to honestly say, he kind of turned my world around that day."

Mark cares about his community, about the people in his life. When he was little, his mother's breast cancer made him understand what it's like to deal with illness. As an adult, he wanted to help his old teacher do it.

Mark also raises money for youth baseball programs in areas that aren't as wealthy as the one where he grew up. He visits sick kids in the hospital, and supports them at ballgames as part of the Make-A-Wish foundation.

Mark is one of those guys who seldom says "no."

Bill Dwyre, the newspaper columnist, summed up what a lot of people think about Mark: "He was raised right."

CHAPTER 17

Sun, Rain, and a Swing Change

The Diamondbacks traded for Mark to add punch to their batting lineup, but he found himself in a situation like the one he left in Anaheim. Arizona's young slugger, Paul Goldschmidt, was coming off a terrific 2013 season. He led the National League with 36 home runs and 125 RBIs, and he was the team's first baseman of the present and future.

So, Mark headed to the outfield again to become an everyday left fielder.

He was comfortable living in the Phoenix area — he had spent every spring training there with the Angels. But now he was playing in the National League, which doesn't have a designated hitter. Mark would be playing defense all the time, and would be facing a lot of

In 2014, Mark joined the National League, as an Arizona Diamondback. His hitting continued to impress, even though an injury shortened his season.

pitchers who were unfamiliar. Once again, he would have to get comfortable in a new zone.

It didn't take him long.

The 2014 season started very much like Mark's rookie season, when he got a hit in eight of his first 10 games. This time, they weren't just hits, they were boomers. He homered five times in his first nine games and drove in 13 runs to make a great first impression on his new teammates.

It looked like he would pick up right where he left off after setting career highs in homers and RBIs in his last season with the Angels. But since spring training, he had played with a sore right foot, and the pain got much worse in late April.

Mark was running in the outfield at Chicago's Wrigley Field when he felt what he thought was a cramp in his foot. Soon, he could barely run at all. Doctors said he had a stress fracture, which is a tiny crack or a bruise within a bone. Mark's injury forced him to stop playing ball for nearly three months.

It was the first time as a pro that he had missed so much time because of an injury. In his first season with the Diamondbacks, Mark played only 88 of the 162 regular season games. He had 14 home runs and 61 RBIs in 328 at-bats. The last number sounds like a lot, but if he had been able to play the whole season, his stats suggest that Mark could have had 26 home runs and a career-high 115 RBIs.

"I know when I went on the disabled list, I was leading the league in home runs, and maybe in RBI, too," Mark says. "I was probably well on my way to putting together a year similar to what I did in Anaheim."

The 2015 season did not start quite as well, and soon Mark was on the move again. The Diamondbacks needed a catcher, and the Seattle Mariners, an American League club, needed somebody to be the designated hitter, as well as play in the outfield part of the time. The deal was made in the middle of the season, on June 2, and Mark was caught totally by surprise.

He was called into the front office minutes after the D-backs, as the Arizona team is known, had won a close game against the Atlanta Braves. Team executives were waiting for him.

"They said, 'We're a catcher short,'" Mark remembers. "It was that moment of, Oh my God, where am I going? Because there was nothing. No rumors. No rumblings. No nothing."

There's a big difference between a trade that happens during the winter and one that happens during the season. In the offseason, a player has weeks or months to prepare for the move, and to become more familiar with a new team. During the season, he has maybe a day to pack before jumping on a plane to a new city.

"That was the hardest one for me," Mark says of the move to Seattle. "The game is the same, and the desire to play is the same, but you have to move your entire life in the matter of a day."

After being traded from the D-backs to the Mariners, Mark was starting to feel at home in Seattle. But he wouldn't be there long.

It wasn't about the city. After the shock of the news wore off, Mark actually was relieved. He knew Seattle from his years with the Angels, competing against the Mariners regularly in the same American League division. Because he's a musician, Mark also liked the city's reputation as a cool rock-and-roll town.

But he didn't really know anyone on the team and — this time — he wasn't coming off the best season of his career. It was time to make another first impression.

That's harder for some people than others, and Mark is one of them. He's not unfriendly, just quiet. His grade-school teachers remember him as reserved, even as the popular boy who was the best player in Little League.

Mark says that he seldom starts a conversation, so walking in cold to the Mariners' clubhouse was tough.

"I didn't feel very comfortable for a while there," he remembers. "I really had no friends on the team at that time. I ended up making some really good friends ..., but at the time you don't really know, so you have to figure it out."

That took a while. Mark got off to a so-so start, hitting only one home run in his first five weeks with the Mariners. His batting average slipped into the .220s. He knew he needed help.

All along his road from T-ball to MLB, Mark had people who helped him understand the game and its many parts. Some were more than just coaches; they were "mentors," or people who not only teach, but who also advise. A good mentor can make a difficult time easier.

Fortunately, Mark was in a place where he found one. His mentor in Seattle was one of baseball's great pure hitters.

Edgar Martinez played 18 seasons in the major leagues. He was named to the All-Star team seven times, and won seven Silver Slugger awards as the best designated hitter in the league. He was one of the best designated hitters of all time, a role that Mark was finding himself in more often with each season.

"I was always a big fan of him," Mark says. "He was a great hitter ... a great right-handed hitter. Every year, he was putting up great numbers, and it just looked like he knew exactly what [pitch] was coming. It was fun to watch."

Nobody likes to ask for help. But Mark swallowed his pride and went to Edgar, who was the Mariners' hitting coach.

"I said, basically, 'Look man, I'm lost. I've been doing this for a while, but I'm not going very well right now. Tell me what you think I should do.'"

Edgar had been retired as a player for about 10 years, but he was able to connect with Mark. He didn't tell Mark what to do. He showed him.

They would go to the indoor batting cage together, and work with a pitching machine or one of the team's batting practice pitchers. Major league clubs have machines that can throw just about any kind of pitch, not just fastballs.

"I used to just give him the bat and say, 'How do you hit this pitch?' and he was still totally able to get in there and demonstrate it," Mark says.

"I would go home and copy it. In batting practice, copy it, and just have faith that if this worked for him it's going to work for me. I think that was a big step for me, pride-wise."

Mark remembered how he had come back from similar struggles in the minor leagues, at Double-A Arkansas. He came back here, too.

After batting a puny .134 in June, he stopped digging, and climbed out of his hole. He finished the season with a .262 average, 22 home runs, and 64 RBIs. Not fantastic, but respectable.

Although 2015 wasn't one of his best years, Mark is very proud of how he asked for and accepted help, and how he turned the season around.

"For me, as a player, I overcame a pretty big obstacle," he says. "Some people categorized it as a down year. You can say what you want, but I don't look at it that way."

Finally, Mark was feeling at home in Seattle when — six days before the end of the 2015 season — the Mariners fired their general manager and hired former Angels' GM Jerry DiPoto.

Can you figure out what happened next?

CHAPTER 18

The Oriole Soars Into Home Run History

On the field, Mark finally felt like himself again. He liked Seattle, with its music culture and youthful energy. It might be the kind of place he could call home.

The Mariners didn't have a very good year in 2015. Even with the offseason addition of slugger Nelson Cruz — who had won the major league home run title with the Orioles in 2014 — and the late-season surge by Mark, they finished in fourth place. They fired their general manager during the last week of the season.

The new general manager wasn't new to Mark, of course. Jerry DiPoto was the GM who uprooted him in Anaheim, trading him to the Arizona Diamondbacks in 2013. History was about to repeat itself.

Mark was expected to earn about $9 million in 2016. DiPoto must have thought the Mariners could spend that money better. So he traded Mark and a pitcher to the Baltimore Orioles for a little-known catcher, Steve Clevenger.

The move was clearly a salary dump, a way to save money for the future. Mark was a big-time power hitter, and only once in his six-year career had Clevenger appeared in more than 35 major league games.

"When I called [Mark], I actually told him not to take this the wrong way," DiPoto told the media after the trade. "He's a great guy, he brings a lot of skill to the table, and it's always difficult to trade right-handed power, but there are reasons for everything."

Mark has always said that he never took the trade personally. But because of what happened the next year, you have to wonder how much he enjoyed showing the Mariners what they were missing.

He was an important acquisition for the Orioles, because they were in danger of losing two-time major league home run king Chris Davis to an offer from another team. So Mark provided a power bat to fill the gap if he left.

But Chris stayed with the Orioles, so the addition of Mark sent them into the 2016 season with two big-time power hitters in a lineup that also included an exciting center fielder, Adam Jones, and budding stars Manny Machado and Jonathan Schoop.

Mark wasn't thinking about any of that when DiPoto

called him about the move. All he knew then was that he had been traded for the third time in fewer than two years, and it didn't feel good.

"That was hard, too," he says. "I thought I was just hitting my stride in Seattle. I was really starting to perform well, and I was quite happy. Then I got traded again, and Baltimore was a team that I never, ever thought about playing for."

Baltimore's nickname is "Charm City," but there was nothing charming about what was going on there in 2015. The city had been rocked by rioting after the ugly, police-related death in April of a young man named Freddie Gray. Unrest near Oriole Park forced two games against the Chicago White Sox to be postponed.

The last game of that series had to be played with the stadium gates locked, and without any fans — the city could not spare the police it thought were needed to keep them safe. It was a huge news story that day, and every sports fan in the country was talking about it.

Today, that game is known as the "No-Fan Game." It was so quiet that the players could hear the radio and TV announcers way up in the second deck talking about them while they were on the field. At one point, Adam Jones was up to bat, and he stepped out of the batter's box to yell something up at the broadcasters.

The tragedy of Freddie Gray sparked a dramatic rise in violence on the streets of Baltimore. But when Mark learned that he was going there, it wasn't the city's bad reputation that disappointed him. It was the geography.

Mark sprints to first base after making contact at the plate.

"No disrespect," he says. "It's just an East Coast team and I'm a West Coast guy, and I didn't know anything about it. I'd been there a handful of times as a visiting player, got a few hits, and didn't know much else."

When he arrived at the Orioles spring training camp in Sarasota, Florida, he was pleasantly surprised. He didn't feel like an outsider, like he did in Seattle, even though Seattle is a West Coast city. He walked into the clubhouse, and its mix of young and veteran players welcomed him.

"I got here and I said, Hey, they've got something going on. Got some good things going. These guys get it," he says. "I think because I felt comfortable, I was able to go out and produce and play well."

Mark had gotten off to a great start during his first full season with the Angels in 2011, and he did the same when he opened the 2014 season in Arizona. He struggled after the midseason trade to Seattle, but here he made another great first impression.

On Opening Day 2016 against the Minnesota Twins, Mark had four hits. He hit safely in 17 of his first 19 games as an Oriole, and finished the month of April with a .337 batting average, six homers, and 19 RBIs. Very big numbers.

He would have played first base full time if Chris Davis had left. Instead, he played 95 games in right field and 59 games as the designated hitter.

Looking back, he gives a lot of credit to his teammates for making things much easier than they were after his other two trades. Most of the veterans on the team had been traded at some point, and they knew the value of bonding quickly with a new teammate.

"Guys have been through it before, and kind of paved the way," Mark says. "It was like, 'Hey, you're new here but we're all in this together.'"

If Mark was a backup plan in case the Orioles had lost Chris Davis, the plan paid off, even though Chris did sign a huge, seven-year contract that year.

Until 2016, Mark's best home run year was 2013, when he hit 34. On Aug. 18, 2016, he blew by that number, hitting a 3-run shot against the Houston Astros for his 35th homer of the year.

There would be many more homers to come in a season in which he had a lot of big hits and big games. One of those games was against the Texas Rangers, when Mark hit two homers in one inning. It was the first time an Oriole had done that. In his 10th game as an Oriole, Mark drove in five runs. He drove in at least three runs in a game 13 times over the course of the season.

In the last eight games of the regular season, he hit four home runs while the Orioles were sewing up their third playoff spot in five years. Mark had never been on a playoff team, and in 2016, he was a big part of his team's success.

The Friday night at Yankee Stadium when Mark hit his last regular-season homer was a special moment, a career moment. It made him the MLB home run king of 2016.

After reaching third base, Mark takes a leadoff during a game against the Angels.

But Mark was more focused on how that series with the Yankees would affect the playoffs.

The Orioles had locked up a spot, but they had to win all three games against the Yanks to get home field advantage in the American League wild card game.

The O's blew out the Yankees on Friday, 8-1, powered by a sixth inning in which Mark, Adam Jones, and Jonathan Schoop each hit home runs. The next day, Mark had four hits in a 7-3 loss. In the final game of the series and the regular season, he scored a run that helped the Orioles win.

It was a great series, especially for Mark, but without the sweep — winning all the games in the series — they had to travel to Toronto to play only one game against the Blue Jays. The winner would advance in the playoffs, and the loser would go home.

The game was intense. Low-scoring. The Blue Jays took a 1-run lead in the second inning. The Orioles took the lead in the fourth. The Jays tied it in the fifth, and it stayed that way for a long time.

The game went into extra innings. Finally, in the 11th inning, Jays' slugger Edwin Encarnación hit a dramatic home run.

Just like that the season was over. The Orioles went home.

"It would have been nice to play that game in Camden Yards," Mark says, referring to the name of the Orioles' ballpark. "Who knows if it would have turned out differently, but it is something you won't forget."

During warmups before a game in May 2018, Mark signs balls for his young fans.

No one will forget one thing about that game — Mark supplied *all* of the Orioles' offense, with a 2-run homer that gave them that fourth-inning lead.

Before that season, Orioles' Manager Buck Showalter saw Mark only from a distance. He knew that Mark had tremendous power, but he didn't know for sure how he would do against the tough pitching in the American League East.

He found out fast. So did all those great pitchers.

"It's fun to watch him square up a ball," Showalter said recently, "because it's pretty."

Like everyone, Mark remembers single moments and single years, including 2016, when he hit more homers than anybody in the big leagues. But he also has a big-picture sense of his job.

"You don't remember all that much from individual seasons," he says. "You get an overall feeling of how it was, and then you'll remember some of the good times, maybe some of the good games. I think more than anything else, you remember the people."

AFTERWORD

Shortly after he was traded to Arizona in 2014, Mark met Maile Krauss when the Diamondbacks were on a road trip to San Francisco. They have been together ever since.

Maile (pronounced *My-lee*) was working in the advertising industry. Mark was adjusting to his new team, and to a new league.

Maile went to college in Washington, D.C., but she grew up in Northern California. She's tall, which is always good when you're a volleyball player, like she was. She loves sports and music, so Mark and Maile have a lot in common.

On Dec. 16, 2017, they were married near Mark's home in Southern California. Hank Conger was a groomsman.

Mark had always put baseball before anything else in his life. That's why he waited until he was almost 32 years

In December 2017, Mark married Maile Krauss, who shares his love of sports and music.

old to get married, and to think about starting a family.

"The first couple years when you're in the major leagues, there's a lot going on and there are a lot of unknowns and a lot of stress," Mark says. "It was easier for me to focus on the baseball.

"Obviously, things have changed." He smiles.

Maile says that when they got married, Mark was seeking "balance." He dabbled in other interests — playing music, collecting vintage guitars — but he wanted, as adults like to say, to "settle down."

On their honeymoon, they went to England and Spain, but they didn't just see the sights like most tourists.

They went in search of a rare Gibson guitar from 1960 that Mark hoped to add to his collection.

"We were on a quest," Maile says, "and we brought home a piece of history."

"It's something we will have always and forever," she says, "and it's a fun way to remember our honeymoon."

When Maile talks about "balance," it's with an eye to the future. Mark has accomplished a lot in the big leagues, and if he doesn't get injured, he can play for many more years. (He sat out more than a month in the 2018 season with a thigh injury.) But at some point, he will stop playing ball altogether.

In the years she has known him, Maile says she has seen Mark come out of his shell. He gets a lot of satisfaction, she says, from helping the younger players on his team. He had so many good coaches that he might become one himself.

Maile Trumbo says that only recently has Mark gotten comfortable with success, realizing "how cool it all is."

"I really do like talking hitting," Mark says. "At some point I can imagine trying to get back into it as a coach, but I think for a while after [my playing career] ... it would probably be good to do some of the things I missed out on."

Today, Mark seems to be having more fun playing baseball than at any time since he was a kid.

"I'm really proud of him," Maile says. "Even in his first year with the Orioles — when he did so well — he wasn't able to stop and appreciate how cool it all is."

The Trumbos are looking forward to having kids, which makes Mark think a lot about his own childhood. He thinks a lot about Grant's "tough love" and narrow focus on baseball.

"It was an old-school approach, and that's what he thought would work," Mark says.

Mark plays the vintage guitar he and Maile discovered during their honeymoon in Europe.

And it did work. But Mark wonders about another way.

"I don't have kids yet," he says, "but I've always thought about what … the ideal parent-coach looks like. It's hard to define, exactly, what kind of role you should have."

He also wonders if he would be an even better baseball player if he also had played basketball and football in high school. He was big enough. He was athletic enough.

He played both sports through middle school, and basketball especially fit his size and abilities.

But he gave it up to compete in baseball year-round.

All the work he did as a youngster made him the major leaguer he is today, but Mark has a little different outlook about kids and sports from his dad's.

He believes in playing lots of different sports. "I think it's good for kids."

He values the time his parents and his coaches gave to him. It helped him develop good habits, on the field and in school.

"I think the one thing they had in common was a hard-work mentality," he says.

He notes that today, little kids sometimes are rewarded just for showing up.

"This might be unpopular," he says, but when he was really young, "it wasn't [that] everyone got a trophy."

"If you're constantly told you're doing great, and you're not, the real world is not that forgiving. You're going to have to earn it."

People look at Mark and see a big man who is one of the strongest players in the major leagues.

Mark looks at people and sees many kinds of strength. To him, it isn't about size, or even sports. It's about believing in yourself, even when life makes that hard. It's about the people who help you, and keeping them close.

MARK TRUMBO

By the Numbers
2010 through 2017

The language of baseball is statistics. People describe players by their numbers — how many home runs they hit, how many bases they steal, how many wins and losses a pitcher has... The language of numbers can seem foreign, but statistics communicate how good players are.

Year	Team	LG	G	AB	R	H	TB	2B	3B	HR	RBI	BB	IBB	SO	SB
2010	LAA	AL	8	15	2	1	1	0	0	0	2	1	0	8	0
2011	LAA	AL	149	539	65	137	257	31	1	29	87	25	6	120	9
2012	LAA	AL	144	544	66	146	267	19	3	32	95	36	3	153	4
2013	LAA	AL	159	620	85	145	281	30	2	34	100	54	6	184	5
2014	ARI	NL	88	328	37	77	136	15	1	14	61	28	3	89	2
2015 [-] 2 teams -			142	508	62	133	228	23	3	22	64	36	1	132	0
2015	SEA	AL	96	334	39	88	140	13	0	13	41	26	1	93	0
2015	ARI	NL	46	174	23	45	88	10	3	9	23	10	0	39	0
2016	BAL	AL	159	613	94	157	327	27	1	47	108	51	1	170	2
2017	BAL	AL	146	559	79	131	222	22	0	23	65	42	0	149	1

Team — LAA (Los Angeles Angels of Anaheim); ARI (Arizona Diamondbacks);
SEA (Seattle Mariners); BAL (Baltimore Orioles)
LG—league; G—games; AB—at-bats; R—runs scored; H—hits; TB—total bases;
2B—doubles; 3B—triples; HR—home runs; RBI—runs batted in; BB—bases on balls (walks);
IBB—intentional bases on balls (intentional walks); SO—strikeouts; SB—stolen bases;
CS—caught stealing; AVG—batting average; OBP—on-base percentage;
SLG—slugging percentage; OPS—on-base percentage plus slugging percentage

CS	AVG	OBP	SLG	OPS
0	.067	.125	.067	.192
4	.254	.291	.477	.768
5	.268	.317	.491	.808
2	.234	.294	.453	.747
3	.235	.293	.415	.707
0	.262	.310	.449	.759
0	.263	.316	.419	.735
0	.259	.299	.506	.805
0	.256	.316	.533	.850
0	.234	.289	.397	.686

Statistics courtesy of MLB.com

GARY AMBROSE

GLOSSARY

OF BASEBALL TERMS

ACE — Best or winningest starting pitcher on a team.

AROUND THE HORN — Practice of players throwing the ball around the infield after recording an out and no one is on base.

AT-BAT — A player's turn to hit.

BACKSTOP — Fence or wall behind home plate, usually topped with a net or screen, to protect fans from wild pitches and foul balls. Also, a slang term for catcher.

BALK — Umpire's call when a pitcher starts a throwing motion toward home plate and either stops or throws to a base in an attempt to pick off a runner, and when a pitcher stumbles or makes a false move intended to fool the runner. When a balk is called, each base runner moves up one base. The batter does not advance.

BASES LOADED — Runners are on all three bases.

BATTING AVERAGE — Percentage of the number of hits measured against the number of times at bat over a defined period; expressed as three digits.

BATTING CAGE — Fence or net enclosure in which batters practice hitting — on the field in a stadium, in an enclosed tunnel under the stands, or at a commercial batting facility.

BATTING ORDER — Order in which a coach or manager assigns batters to hit (see: *lineup*).

BASE COACHES — Persons stationed in foul territory outside first and third base to tell base runners whether to stop or run to the next base/home plate. The third base coach also signals what hitters at the plate should do.

BLOOP/BLOOPER — Soft hit that falls between the infielders and outfielders. Also called a Texas Leaguer.

BREAKING BALL — Pitch that drops or curves at or before reaching home plate (also: *curveball*).

BULLPEN — Confined area in the stadium where relief pitchers warm up on practice mounds, usually beyond the outfield.

BUNT — Batter's attempt to move a runner on base to the next base by pushing the ball with the bat held parallel to the ground, not by swinging through the ball. Successful bunts drop before reaching the pitcher, first, or third baseman. A bunt does not count as an at-bat, and the bunter expects to be thrown out at first (see: *sacrifice*). Sometimes, hitters bunt without runners on base to fool fielders. If successful, it's a hit. If not, an at-bat is charged.

CALLED UP — Promoted from the minor leagues to the majors.

CATCHER'S INTERFERENCE — When a catcher's glove comes in contact with a hitter's swing, the batter is awarded first base.

CATCHER'S SIGNS — Hand signals the catcher makes crouching behind the plate to tell the pitcher which kind of pitch to throw (see: *sign*).

CAUGHT STEALING — When a base runner attempts to steal a base and the catcher (or, sometimes, other infielder) throws him out (see: *steal*).

CHANGEUP — Pitch that appears to be a fastball but is slower, due to the pitcher's grip, causing the batter to mistime his swing.

CLEANUP HITTER — Player who bats fourth in the lineup. Often the most powerful hitter, and occasionally the best overall hitter on the team. So-called because with a hit, he "cleans up," or advances, the runners on base.

CLOSER — Relief pitcher for the team with the lead, who closes out the late innings of a game.

CLUBHOUSE — Baseball's name for the locker room.

COMMAND — Pitcher's ability to throw the pitch where he wants it to go.

CONTROL — Same as command.

CURVEBALL — See: *breaking ball*.

DELIVERY — Motion with which a pitcher throws.

DESIGNATED HITTER — In the American League only, a player who bats but does not play in the field. He bats instead of the pitcher. In the National League, there is no DH; pitchers bat unless they are removed from the game, and replaced in the batting order with a pinch hitter. When American and National League teams play against each other (interleague play), the DH is used when the American League is the host team, and not if it is the National League.

DIAMOND — Field where the game is played. The infield is a square whose sides are 90 feet. Each right angle is a base (including home plate). The pitching mound in the middle of the square is 60 feet, 6 inches from home plate. Dimensions for the outfield vary among stadiums.

DOUBLEHEADER — Two games between the same teams on the same day. When one game starts in in the morning and the later one at night, it's called a day-night doubleheader.

DOUBLE PLAY — Two outs are made by the defensive team from one batted ball. Most often, it occurs when the batter hits an infield ground ball — the fielder touches or throws to second, and that fielder throws to first before either runner reaches the base.

DRAFT — Selection procedure for major league teams to get rights to young players coming out of school. Teams with the worst win-loss records in the previous season choose — or draft — earliest, and teams with the better records draft later.

DUGOUT — Enclosure on the field facing the diamond where players, the manager, and some coaches stay during games when they're not on the field. Each team has a dugout, one on the first base side, and one on the third base side.

EARNED RUN AVERAGE (ERA) — Measure of a pitcher's effectiveness. The statistic represents the number of earned runs a pitcher allows for every nine innings pitched. The lower the ERA, the better the pitcher. (See: *unearned run*).

ERROR — Fielder misplays a ball that the official scorer says should have been handled to make an out or stop a runner's advance.

FALL CLASSIC — Another name for the World Series.

FARM TEAM — A minor league team (see: *minor leagues*).

FASTBALL — Pitch with the most speed. Thrown either with two fingers across the seams of the ball, to go faster and straighter, or with two fingers on the seams, to move a bit left or right.

FIELDER'S CHOICE — Batter gets safely on base because the fielder chose to make an out on a runner at another base. The batter is not awarded a hit.

FLY BALL — Ball hit into the air; the opposite of a ground ball.

FOUL BALL — Ball hit wide of either right or left field foul lines.

FOUL LINES — Chalk lines extending from home plate to the foul poles in the left field and right field corners. They determine whether batted balls are fair or foul.

FOUL POLE — Poles on either side of the outfield that help umpires determine when a ball is hit fair or foul. If a ball strikes the foul pole, it is a fair ball. If it hits the foul pole above the fence, it is a home run.

FRAMING A PITCH — Catcher moves his glove after receiving a pitch to make it appear to the umpire that it was thrown in the strike zone.

FREE AGENT — Player no longer under contract to a team who is free to make another deal with any other team.

FULL COUNT — Batter has three balls and two strikes.

GOES THE OTHER WAY — Right-handed hitter hits to right field, and a left-handed hitter hits to left field (see: *opposite field hit* and *pull hitter*).

GRAND SLAM — Home run when the bases are loaded, scoring four runs.

GREEN LIGHT — Player who doesn't need permission from a coach to steal a base or swing at a pitch is said to have a green light.

GROUND BALL/GROUNDER — Ball hit on the ground; the opposite of a fly ball.

GROUND RULE DOUBLE — Hit that bounces into the outfield stands or, in some cases, gets stuck in or under the outfield fence. The umpire stops play, and the batter is awarded second base. If another runner was on base at the time of the hit, the umpire determines where, and awards him the base (or home plate) he probably would have reached. Also called an automatic double.

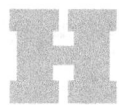

HIT AND RUN — In a strategy to gain an extra base, a coach signals a batter to swing at the next pitch at the same time the base runner is signaled to run to the next base as the pitch is thrown. If the batter gets a hit, the player on base has gotten a head start.

HIT BY PITCH (HBP) — Pitch strikes the batter, who is awarded first base, but is not credited with a hit.

INFIELD FLY RULE — Umpire calls an out before a fly ball drops in or near the infield, and that would have been caught easily. The rule was made to stop a fielder from letting the ball drop solely to retrieve it and force out base runners ahead of the batter. The ruling can be made only with runners on first and second, or with the bases loaded, and with fewer than two outs.

INFIELDER — First, second, and third baseman, and the shortstop.

INNING — A baseball game is nine innings. If the score is tied at the end of nine, there are extra innings until someone wins. There are no ties. Innings are divided in two — the visiting team bats in the top, or first part of the inning, and the home team bats in the bottom, or last part of the inning.

KNOCKDOWN PITCH — Pitcher purposefully throws a ball so close to the batter that he must dive out of the way.

KNUCKLEBALL — Pitch gripped with the knuckles or fingernails so that it doesn't spin. The lack of spin makes the ball subject to air currents, and can move in any direction.

L

LINE DRIVE — Fly ball hit on a straight line, rather than high in the air.

LINEUP — Order in which a coach or manager assigns batters to hit (also: *batting order*).

M

MAJOR LEAGUES — Top U.S. professional level.

MINOR LEAGUES — Lower levels of baseball, where professional prospects, usually young, compete for spots in the major leagues. All major league teams have minor league programs, often called farm systems; prospects sometimes are said to be "down on the farm" (see: *farm team*).

MANAGER — Person in charge of the team who makes on-field decisions. In other sports, he is called the head coach.

MOUND/PITCHING MOUND — Hill 10 inches above the level of the diamond, 60 feet, 6 inches from home plate, from which the pitcher throws to the batter.

NO-HITTER — A complete (nine-inning) game in which the pitcher allows no hits from the opposing team, although there might be base runners due to walks, hit batsmen, or errors such as catcher interference.

ON-BASE PERCENTAGE (OBP) — Percentage of times a player gets on base, compared with the number of times he bats.

ON-BASE PLUS SLUGGING (OPS) — Statistic that combines a player's on-base percentage with his slugging average.

ON DECK/ON-DECK CIRCLE — Batter scheduled to hit after the player at the plate is on deck, who waits in the on-deck circle between the dugout and home plate.

OPPOSITE FIELD HIT — Right-handed batter hits to right field, and a left-handed batter hits to left field (see: *goes the other way* and *pull hitter*).

OUTFIELDER — Left, center, or right fielder.

PASSED BALL — Pitch the catcher should have been able to handle but didn't. A base runner must advance on the play for a passed ball to be called. This is a separate statistic from an error (see: *wild pitch*).

PERFECT GAME — Pitcher's no-hitter in which no player from the opposing team reaches first base.

PICKOFF — Catcher or pitcher catches a base runner too far from the bag and throws him out before he can get back safely.

PINCH HITTER — Player assigned by the manager to bat in place of another player.

PINCH RUNNER — Player assigned by the manager to replace a base runner, usually because he is faster.

PITCHING RUBBER —White strip atop the pitching mound from which the pitcher must begin his delivery.

POSITION PLAYER — Any player other than the pitcher.

PULL HITTER — Left-handed batter who hits mostly to right field, and a right-hander who hits mostly to left field (see: *opposite field hit* and *goes the other way*).

RADAR GUN — Device used by baseball scouts to determine the velocity of pitches. Similar to what police use to catch speeding drivers.

RBI — Run batted in.

RELIEF PITCHER/RELIEVER — Pitcher who enters the game after the starting pitcher is taken out.

ROSIN BAG — Small sack at the back of the pitching mound containing a sticky substance pitchers rub to grip the ball better.

ROTATION/STARTING ROTATION — Schedule of a team's starting pitchers.

SACRIFICE/SACRIFICE FLY — Batter hits a fly ball in fair or foul territory that is caught, but deep enough to allow a base runner to tag his base after the catch and advance to the next base, or home, before the fielder can throw him out. The batter is awarded an RBI if the runner scores, and is not recorded with an at-bat.

SAVE — Relief pitcher who finishes the game earns a save if: he enters the game with his team ahead by no more than three runs and pitches for at least one inning; he holds any lead for at least the last three innings; he enters the game with the potential tying run on base, at the plate, or in the on-deck circle.

THE SHOW — The major leagues.

SIGN — Signal from a coach or manager that directs a base runner to try to steal, or a batter to swing or not, or infielders to arrange themselves a certain way. Pitchers get their signs from catchers, who might get them from the dugout. Signs are hand signals disguised within other hand signals so the opposing team can't tell what's being called.

SLIDER — Relatively fast pitch that tails down and away through the strike zone.

SPLIT-FINGERED FASTBALL — Pitch thrown like a fastball, but with the index and middle finger spread apart to change the spin of the ball, usually to dive down near the plate.

STARTER — First pitcher in the game for each team.

STEAL/STOLEN BASE — Base runner attempts to reach the next base before the pitcher or catcher can throw him out; usually he leaves the base he's on during the pitcher's windup.

SQUEEZE PLAY — With a runner at third base, the batter bunts as the runner leaves for home. If successful, the runner scores before the pitcher or an infielder can retrieve the ball and throw home.

STRIKE ZONE — Imaginary rectangle above home plate extending up from the bottom of the hitter's knees to just below the letters on his jersey.

SWEEP — Team wins all the games in a series against another team.

THE SHOW — The major leagues.

TRIPLE PLAY — Three outs are made on one batted ball.

UMPIRE — Person who make rulings during a game. Four work in major league games — one behind home plate to call balls, strikes, and plays at the plate, and one near each base to rule on the infield and outfield plays nearest to him. All umpires may rule on whether falls are fair or foul.

UNEARNED RUN — Run that scores because of an error and does not count against a pitcher's earned-run average (See: *earned run average*).

UTILITY INFIELDER — Player with skills to play several or all infield positions.

WALK/INTENTIONAL WALK — Batter is awarded first base when he takes four pitches thrown outside the strike zone. Also called a base on balls. Sometimes, a team walks a batter intentionally, signaled by the manager, because the batter on deck is considered a less dangerous hitter, or it wants to put a player on first to set up a possible double play.

WALK-OFF HIT — Game-winning hit that can be achieved only by the home team, because it bats in the bottom of the inning. The moment the run scores, the game ends, and the teams walk off the field.

WILD PITCH — Pitch the catcher cannot reasonably reach and control. A base runner must advance on the play for a wild pitch to be called. This is a separate statistic from an error (see: *passed ball*).

WINDUP — Pitcher's motion before releasing the ball.

WINTER BALL — Offseason competition where major and minor leaguers may play in other countries with warm-weather weather.

www.ingramcontent.com/pod-product-compliance
Lightning Source LLC
Chambersburg PA
CBHW070737020526
44118CB00035B/1475